The Consistency Effect

How to Turn Reliable Actions into Remarkable Results

BRAD J. HENDERSON

Lucky Book Publishing

MY GIFT TO YOU

I am so glad you're here!

As my Gift to you, get FREE access the Audiobook of **The Consistency Effect: How to Turn Reliable Actions into Remarkable Results** by scanning the QR Code below or visiting

https://www.consistency-edge.com/pages/shop

Praise for The Consistency Effect

How to Turn Reliable Actions into Remarkable Results

A Must Read!
This book is a blueprint for success. The takeaways allow the reader to adapt the lessons learned and apply them to their style of management regardless of the industry. By combining emotional intelligence, human connection and real world business challenges, Brad Henderson found the perfect way to simplify what most leaders overthink.

— Sasha Brosseau, Chief Executive Officer Berkshire Hathaway HomeServices Québec

A Real Key to Success!
The Consistency Effect is a brilliant book for both business and personal growth. So many people suffer from comparing themselves and their results to those of others when they should

be writing their OWN success story. Brad's stories and experience are a great reminder that showing up every day taking small, consistent actions in a way that is unique and authentic to you, is the real key to success. I will be reading The Consistency Effect multiple times.

— **Cal Misener, Best selling Author** *"The Freedom Framework - A Business Owner's Guide to Doing More of What They Love and Less of What They Don't"*

Truly inspiring!
Henderson really hit this one out of the park! This book delivers immediate, actionable steps to implement The Consistency Effect. Don't be distracted by trying to become an overnight success. Focus on small, consistent actions that inch you towards success. Clarify your goal, seek out mentors, build community and learn from setbacks. Showing up consistently and doing the work is what wins the game.

— **Fran Garton, Pain Reduction Coach and Author of** *Healing the Hurt: A Step-by-Step Guide to Alleviate and Minimize Pain*

Brilliant!

This isn't just a book; it's a working manual for real-world results. The sheer amount of practical wisdom, no-nonsense advice, and instantly usable concepts means I'll be referring back to it constantly for consistent improvement. The insights are brilliant, and spoiler alert: embracing consistent effort is your ultimate key to success. A must-have for every serious entrepreneur and leader.

— Nick Grauds, Founder & President Con-Frame Ltd

Outstanding Book!

As an executive, I've navigated plenty of leadership and business books — many of which promise grand transformations yet rarely deliver actionable insights. Brad Henderson's The Consistency Effect genuinely stands apart by providing practical, achievable strategies relevant to anyone aiming for meaningful professional growth, whether they're seasoned executives or emerging leaders. Brad's style is clear, relatable, and approachable—even the baseball metaphors land effectively, making complex ideas feel accessible regardless of your familiarity with sports.

If you're looking for a leadership book that delivers realistic, impactful advice grounded in experience, The Consistency Effect is an outstanding choice.

— Kyle Dennhardt, COO & Operating Partner Grey Road Partners

A Genuine Surprise!
Hesitant about business books? Me too. But 'The Consistency Effect' was a genuine surprise. Brad Henderson's conversational style makes it incredibly readable and relatable, even if this isn't your usual genre. While he uses baseball metaphors, they cleverly illustrate his points about consistent effort ('singles') versus grand gestures ('home runs') without needing detailed sports expertise.
What really makes this book stand out are Henderson's personal stories from his impressive, multi-industry career – the wins, the losses, the unexpected pivots (including a fun chapter on his music dreams!). It feels less like a textbook and more like hearing valuable life lessons from a seasoned mentor.

— Anne Hayes, Owner & Publisher Flowerpot Press

An Innovative Approach to your Career!
Is the Consistency Effect a book that can help
you find success in your chosen career path- a
resounding yes? Now if your life plan consists
of buying lottery tickets, visiting casinos and
generally hoping the gods smile on you then you
should probably stop reading now.
What the author Brad Henderson presents is an
innovative approach to your career that ensures
that you will maximize your skills and prepares
you to act decisively when opportunities present
themselves. Drawing from a highly successful
career that spanned over four decades, the
author demonstrates how a consistent and
deliberate approach to your work life is the best
way to realize dreams and ambitions.

**— John O'Bryan, Former Chairman, CBRE
Limited**

Insightful and Practical.
This book beautifully captures the essence of
leadership and personal development through
the lens of simplicity. Brad's ability to distill
complex ideas into impactful phrases is both
insightful and practical, providing readers with
memorable takeaways that can be applied
in various aspects of life and business. I truly

recommend this book to all thought leaders who are looking to expand their business in the right direction!

— Charles Achampong, Best Selling Author, Around The World in Family Days

So Insightful and relatable!
Wow! What an amazing concept. The use of baseball as a metaphor for business and personal development is so engaging and relatable. Brad effectively draws parallels between the two, illustrating how consistency, resilience, and strategic thinking are crucial for success in both fields. This approach makes it very accessible and inspiring for readers from all walks of life. I really enjoyed reading this book!

— Dionne Nicholls-Germain, Bestselling Author, *The 90-Day Conquering Unforgiveness Journal : For High-Performing High Achievers*

A book I will come back to often!
The Consistency Effect inspired me with practical tips and stories, reminding me that steady effort and small wins truly lead to lasting success— something I'll carry forward.

— **Shelley A. Murdock, Author,** *In Search for Longevity* **, Longevity Coach**

What a great read!
The message is awesome and clear. Showing up consistently can lead to success and this recipe to demonstrate the why, is a great read.

— **Heather Colman, Author of** *Our Money Narrative, MBA*

Engaging Practical Guide.
The Consistency Effect is an engaging, practical guide to leadership at any stage. Brad J. Henderson shares a wealth of real-life lessons from his perspective as a career CEO, grounded in resilience, mentorship, and consistent action. His GRAND SLAM framework is clear and inspiring. As a leadership coach, I appreciated his insights on team culture and growth. A favourite line: "Resilience isn't about never falling... It's how you use that experience to move even higher next time." A valuable read for both emerging and experienced leaders.

— **Eden Spodek, Founder & Leadership Coach, Spodek & Co.**

Dedication

This book is a testament to the power of mentorship and the profound impact that guidance can have on one's life journey. It is dedicated with heartfelt gratitude to all those remarkable individuals who have served as beacons of wisdom, inspiration, and support throughout my personal and professional odyssey.

My Dream

The Consistency Effect

When I first made the decision to become a leadership coach, a persistent vision kept me awake at night. I imagined leaders freed from the crushing weight of comparison, finding joy in their own unique journey rather than measuring themselves against sensationalized success stories. I dreamed of workplaces where steady progress was celebrated as much as dramatic breakthroughs, where burnout was replaced by sustainable excellence.

This vision emerged from witnessing a pervasive problem throughout my career across multiple industries. We live in a world obsessed with the extraordinary. Scroll through social media, flip through business magazines, or listen to the news, and you're bombarded with stories of overnight successes, disruptive innovations, and monumental "grand slam" achievements. These narratives are compelling, even addictive. They promise rapid transformation, skipping the messy, often mundane middle part of hard work.

But here's a quiet truth that often gets lost in the noise: real, sustainable success isn't built on grand slams alone. It's built on consistency. It's the steady stream of singles and doubles, the reliable plays made day in and day out, that win games, championships, and build legendary careers. Think of the baseball greats – their enduring legacy isn't defined by one or two home runs, but by years of consistent performance at the plate and in the field.

As a leadership coach, I believed I had valuable insights to share, but my thoughts were scattered without clear organization. I realized that writing *The Consistency Effect* would force me to clarify my thinking and articulate the patterns I'd observed across decades of leadership. What began as a personal exercise in clarity evolved into something more meaningful – my gift to future generations of leaders, a chance for them to learn from both my successes and my mistakes.

My dream for this book extends beyond business strategy – it's about reclaiming the human side of achievement. I envision leaders finding permission to embrace their own pace, to trust in daily disciplines rather than dramatic gestures, and to recognize that consistency itself is an extraordinary quality in a world obsessed with overnight success. This isn't just about building better businesses; it's about building better lives through the quiet power of showing up, day after day, bringing our best to what matters most.

"We are what we repeatedly do. Excellence, then, is not an act, but a habit."

— Aristotle

TABLE OF CONTENTS

Foreword

When a friend of nearly 40 years asks you to write a forward for his book, a number of thoughts go through your mind. As well as being a great honour, it is even more meaningful when you finish the initial read through and realize that it is work of great value and insight. Such was my introduction to *The Consistency Effect*.

"Not another business book," I can hear you shout. What on earth can it say that has not been explored so many times before? Well, *The Consistency Effect* really is different, as is the author Brad Henderson. Brad is definitively not one of the ubiquitous billionaires who feel compelled to write a vanity book in order to tell a rags to riches story that has little connection and even less relevance to the business lives most of us enjoy.

Having worked alongside Brad through large portions of his career, I can attest that he is one of the most skilled managers I have ever encountered.

He has an uncanny ability to understand how organizations work and develop client solutions that are innovative and industry leading. Brad offers practical insights from a highly successful career that has spanned multiple industries and from a personal life that has presented its share of challenges.

Having read hundreds of business books throughout my career, I can confidently say that *The Consistency Effect* stands apart in significant ways. While many authors champion dramatic change and disruptive innovation, Brad makes a compelling case for the underrated power of showing up consistently, delivering quality work, and accumulating small wins that compound over time.

The Consistency Effect is not only an engaging read; it is a book you can return to time and again for advice and perspective. One of the greatest skills we need to develop in our business lives is how to manage our time and effort effectively. As new generations enter the workforce, each with their unique identifying letter, there seems to be a shared desire to achieve the elusive work-life balance. This book doesn't just explore this journey but provides successful strategies to help each reader achieve their own individual goals.

Whether you're early in your career, navigating a professional transition, or leading an organization, you'll find valuable insights within these pages. His candid reflections on both triumphs and setbacks offer lessons that can only come from lived experience.

On a personal note, having survived and thrived for over 50 years in the commercial real estate world, I have come to realize that the most valuable trait all successful people share is an insatiable desire to continue learning. This book is an invaluable addition to that learning journey and one that will continue to offer valuable insights throughout your own career path.

John C. O'Bryan
Former Chairman
CBRE Limited

Pre-game:
Setting the Stage for Success

"Someone is sitting in the shade today because
someone planted a tree a long time ago"
— Warren Buffett.

In the grand stadium of business success, we often find ourselves mesmerized by the spectacular home runs and grand slams – those rare, extraordinary achievements that catapult companies and individuals into the stratosphere of fame and fortune. These are the stories that dominate headlines, inspire countless business books, and fuel the dreams of aspiring entrepreneurs. The Bill Gates, Steve Jobs, and Elon Musks of the world become our idols, their exceptional journeys the gold standard against which we measure our own progress.

But as I reflect on my four-decade journey through the corporate world, from my humble beginnings as a summer intern to my roles as CEO and senior executive across diverse industries, I've come to realize that these headline-grabbing moments, while inspiring, often overshadow a more attainable and equally valuable path to success. This realization is the driving force behind The Consistency Effect.

My goal is to reframe the narrative of success. I want to re-examine the problem of what I believe is misaligned expectations and undue pressure by offering a more attainable, sustainable, and ultimately more fulfilling approach to career and personal development. Drawing on my vast experiences – from managing multi-million-dollar companies to leading international teams of thousands, from driving strategic initiatives in industry-leading companies to building scalable infrastructures in scrappy start-ups – I aim to demonstrate that true success is not about swinging for the fences every time you're at bat. Instead, it's about developing the skills, mindset, and habits that allow you to consistently get on base and advance your position.

A Personal Journey of Discovery

If you indulge me, I will frequently use this particularly apt baseball metaphor to illustrate my core business principle. My own career has been less about hitting home runs and more about consistently getting on base. From my early days in commercial real estate at A.E. LePage (now Cushman & Wakefield) as a wide-eyed summer student, I learned the fundamental power of consistency. The bustling office, filled with the chatter of phone calls and the rustle of papers, was both intimidating and exhilarating. It was here that I first glimpsed how the superstars, the most successful agents, built their client relationships not through grandiose gestures, but through reliable, day-to-day excellence.

As I advanced to managing a team of Canada's elite commercial real estate brokers, I faced new challenges that tested my leadership skills. I quickly had to learn how to motivate high performers, mediate conflicts, and create an environment where everyone could thrive. This role taught me the crucial importance of consistent communication, fair treatment, and leading by example. I realized that effective leadership wasn't about sporadic grand gestures, but about showing up every day with the same level of commitment and integrity.

My career took an unexpected turn when I was offered the position of President at Arqana Technologies, a nimble value-added reseller (VAR) whose business was to purchase IT equipment from manufacturers, enhance it with additional services including integration, installation, customization, or consulting, and sell the complete solution to end customers. This shift from the established world of real estate to the fast-paced, ever-changing landscape of technology was jarring. The familiar rhythms of property cycles were replaced by the frenetic pulse of tech innovation. However, I found that understanding the underlying product or service of a company was secondary to the principle of consistency that had served me well in real estate and was equally valuable in this new context. This experience taught me the universality of consistent performance and the importance of adaptability in applying these principles to new industries.

The acquisition of Arqana by TELUS presented a new set of challenges. Suddenly, I was back in the world of large corporations, but this time with a unique perspective gained from my experience in a smaller, more agile company. The transition was not easy – merging cultures, aligning goals, and navigating corporate hierarchies presented daily challenges. It was during this period that I came to believe it wasn't that people didn't know what to do but rather they didn't do what they knew. By consistently applying the lessons I'd learned about adaptability and incremental improvement, I bridged the gap between the start-up mentality of Arqana and the structured approach of TELUS.

At TELUS, my role also took on new dimensions as I was tasked with turning around underperforming units and driving transformation across diverse business units. These experiences reinforced my belief in the effectiveness of consistent principles: assess thoroughly, plan strategically, execute consistently, and always look for ways to improve.

My time at TELUS also taught me the value of versatility in leadership. Each division I worked with presented unique challenges, requiring me to adapt my approach while staying true to core principles. It showed me that a leader's toolkit must be both deep and broad – deep in foundational skills and broad in its applicability across different contexts. The ability to turn around underperforming units became not just a skill, but a defining aspect of my professional identity.

Opportunity created another unexpected turn into the world of robotics and cloud computing when I was recruited to NuTech Engineering as president. This leap required me to rapidly acquire new technical knowledge while applying the universal principles of effective leadership I'd honed over the years. The pace was relentless and the learning curve steep, but the experience was invaluable. I learned that consistent growth often means pushing beyond your comfort zone and embracing new challenges with enthusiasm. This period reinforced my belief that the fundamentals of good leadership and consistent performance are applicable across even the most diverse industries.

Life has a way of coming full circle, and I soon found myself back in the familiar territory of commercial real estate, but on a much grander scale. Leading global teams at industry giants CBRE and Cushman & Wakefield was like coming home, but to a home that had significantly changed. The principles were the same, but the scope was global, and the stakes were higher. Here, the importance of consistency was magnified. With teams spread across different time zones and cultures, maintaining a cohesive vision and consistent quality of service was paramount. This experience taught me how to scale the principles of consistency and apply them on a global level.

The culmination of this diverse journey was my role leading the luxury real estate market at Sotheby's International Realty Canada. This position allowed me to blend the commercial acumen I'd developed over the years with a deep appreciation for exceptional client service. It was here that I fully realized how the principles of consistency and incremental improvement could be applied to create truly extraordinary experiences. In the luxury market, where expectations are exceptionally high, the consistent delivery of excellence is not just important – it's essential.

This career arc taught me that success is about taking consistent steps forward, adapting to new environments while staying true to core principles, and always being willing to learn and grow. It's a lesson I've carried with me through every role, every challenge, and every success – and one that I'm passionate about sharing with others as an executive coach as they navigate their own career paths. Consistency and incremental improvement are my guiding stars and their impact on my life incalculable.

The Problem: Misaligned Expectations and Undue Pressure

Why this book? The answer lies in a pervasive problem I've observed throughout my journey across industries. Too often, I've seen talented individuals become discouraged or disillusioned because they measure their success against the extraordinary stories of overnight billionaires or disruptive start-ups that dominate business literature. They overlook the value of their own consistent efforts and incremental achievements, falsely believing that anything short of a "grand slam" is somehow inadequate.

This mindset creates unnecessary pressure and anxiety, leading many to either burn out in pursuit of unrealistic goals or give up entirely, believing they don't have what it takes to succeed. It's a widespread issue that stifles potential, undermines confidence, and robs individuals and organizations of the joy and satisfaction that comes from steady growth and consistent performance.

Moreover, this fixation on exceptional success stories often leads to a skewed perception of what it takes to build a successful career. It encourages unnecessary risk-taking, neglect of fundamental business principles, and a failure to appreciate the power of compounded small wins over time.

The Solution: Reframing Success and Embracing Consistency

I'll address this problem through sharing stories, strategies, and insights gleaned from my own journey and those of others I've encountered along the way. I'll illustrate how the principles of steady performance apply in the business world.

The Power of Consistency: A Deep Dive

Throughout the book, we'll explore several key themes that form the backbone of The Consistency Effect:

SMALL WINS

We'll delve into the psychology of progress and how recognizing and celebrating small achievements can fuel motivation and lead to significant long-term success. I'll share techniques I've used throughout my career to break down large goals into manageable daily actions, and how this approach has led to some of my most significant achievements.

RESILIENCE AND ADAPTABILITY

I'll share techniques for staying relevant and thriving amidst constant change by exploring how to successfully transition your career and the lessons learned along the way.

CONTINUOUS LEARNING AND SKILL DEVELOPMENT

How to cultivate a growth mindset and build a personal curriculum for ongoing professional development. I'll share my own lifelong learning journey.

BUILD AND LEVERAGE PROFESSIONAL NETWORKS EFFECTIVELY.

I'll share insights on creating meaningful connections and nurturing relationships that can open doors and create opportunities throughout your career. We'll explore how networking can play a crucial role in career transitions.

THE ROLE OF MENTORSHIP

We'll explore the impact of both being mentored and mentoring others, and how these relationships can accelerate personal and professional development.

MAINTAINING WORK-LIFE BALANCE

I will outline techniques for maintaining work-life balance and personal fulfillment and building a successful career without sacrificing personal well-being and relationships. I'll be candid about the struggles I've faced in this area and the lessons I've learned about creating a sustainable work-life integration.

BUILDING A STRONG PERSONAL BRAND

The value of consistent effort in building a strong personal brand: We'll examine how day-to-day actions and attitudes contribute to your professional reputation – your brand – and long-term career prospects.

LEADERSHIP LESSONS FOR FOSTERING CONSISTENCY IN TEAMS AND ORGANIZATIONS

I'll share insights from my executive roles on how to create cultures of consistent high performance and continuous improvement.

OVERCOMING SETBACKS: FAILURES ARE STEPPING STONES.

Using examples from my own career transitions and challenges, we'll discuss how to maintain consistency even when faced with obstacles and disappointments. I'll be open about some of my biggest failures and how they ultimately contributed to my success.

A New Perspective on Success

The Consistency Effect is not just about business strategy; it's a guide to building a sustainable and satisfying professional life. It's a reminder that every small action, every minor improvement, every incremental step forward is a victory worth celebrating.

In baseball, even the greatest players fail more often than they succeed. A .300 batting average – getting a hit 3 out of 10 times at bat – is considered excellent. The same principle applies in business and in life. It's not about being perfect; it's about showing up consistently, learning from every at-bat, and steadily improving your game.

Welcome to *The Consistency Effect* – a guide to winning in business and life, one base hit at a time.

Warm-up

The Power of Simplicity:
Distilling Wisdom into Words

"Things should be made as simple as possible, but not simpler" — Albert Einstein.

In the world of leadership and personal development, there's an undeniable magic in simplicity. I have always been drawn to the power of pithy, succinct phrases that pack a punch far beyond their word count. These linguistic gems have the remarkable ability to condense years of experience and insight into a handful of words that resonate deeply and stick in our minds.

Throughout my journey as a leader, coach, and mentor, I've collected these pearls of wisdom like treasures.

But more than clever phrases, they've become the cornerstone of how I share knowledge with others. How I try to make them think.

The process of distilling complex ideas into these bite-sized nuggets of wisdom is an art form. It requires a deep understanding of the subject matter, coupled with the ability to identify its essence. When done well, these phrases become catalysts for learning and change, sparking "aha" moments and shifting perspectives in ways that lengthy explanations often fail to achieve.

In my coaching practice, I use these phrases as a launch pad for the point I intend to share. They are high-level frameworks where more detail can be added with particular reference to a specific situation. These phrases also serve as reminders and triggers to reinforce the learning.

With that in mind, I would like to add two other quotes that resonate: "You have to learn from other people's mistakes because you cannot live long enough to make them all yourself," by Eleanor Roosevelt and "It is more important to be reminded than to be instructed," often attributed to Dr. Samuel Johnson, an 18th-century English writer.

Let's finish this section with the master of insightful quotations, Confucius, who observed that "The true gentleman does not preach what he practices till he has practiced what he preaches." In writing this book, not only was I reminded of many things I've come to embrace in my life, but I also realized there were some things I was not practicing. Rest assured; once I was reminded, I stepped up my game.

Taking the Field - Let's Play Ball!

"Baseball is 90% mental and the other half is physical."
— Yogi Berra

Welcome to the world of baseball, a sport that's as much about strategy and patience as it is about physical skill.

The Long Game: A baseball season is a marathon, not a sprint. Teams play 162 games in a regular season, stretching from spring to fall. This long-term perspective mirrors the journey of building a successful business. Just as a baseball team can't rely on a single great game to win the season, a business or individual can't sustain itself on one big success.

Consistency is Key: In baseball, the most valuable players aren't always the ones hitting home runs. Often, it's the players who consistently get on base with singles and doubles who drive the team's success. Similarly, in business, consistent small wins and steady growth often lead to long-term success and stability.

Bouncing Back: Baseball teams face losses and setbacks throughout the season. The key to success is resilience – the ability to shake off a bad game and come back strong the next day. This mirrors the entrepreneurial journey, where setbacks are inevitable, but the ability to learn and bounce back is crucial.

The World Series: The pinnacle of baseball achievement is reaching and winning the World Series. It's the culmination of a season's worth of hard work, strategy, and perseverance. In the business world, this could be likened to becoming an industry leader, achieving sustainable profitability, or realizing your long-term vision for your company.

The Baseball-Business Connection: Just as a baseball player or team can't rely solely on swinging for the fences and hoping for grand slams, a businessperson shouldn't pin all their or their company's hopes on game-changing breakthroughs. While these big wins are exciting, it's the consistent "singles and doubles" – the small, steady achievements – that often lead to lasting success.

Remember, every grand slam hitter in baseball still celebrates their singles and doubles. In the same way, while we admire the Bill Gates and Elon Musks of the business world, there's immense value and success in building a stable, profitable business through consistent effort and incremental gains.

In both baseball and business, the key is to keep stepping up to the plate, adapting your strategy, and giving it your best shot. Sometimes you'll strike out, sometimes you'll hit it out of the park, but it's the overall performance across many "at-bats" that ultimately determines your success.

1st Inning

The Game of Business: Batting Averages and Success

"The way to win is to work, work, work and have a few insights" — Charlie Munger

---

The Singles and Doubles Player

In the past, when asked about my career and successes, I summed it up by describing myself as more of a singles and doubles kind of player. No dramatic home runs or grand slams – just steady hits that keep the game moving. And you know what? It's worked out pretty well for me.

So, I decided to lean into this comparison. After all, baseball is one of those rare things that most folks understand.

Measuring Success: More than Fancy Math and Big Numbers

OK, so I am going to mix my sports metaphors (and possibly incur the wrath of sports purists everywhere). I'm throwing football wisdom into our baseball-business mix. The great Vince Lombardi, the legendary American football coach once said, "Everyone plays harder when they're keeping score."

So, let's talk about keeping score in business. In baseball, they've got batting average. "How often does this guy actually hit the ball when he's not busy adjusting his cap or spitting sunflower seeds?"

In the business world, we don't have official statisticians tracking our every move (thank goodness). But the concept still applies. We're all trying to figure out how often we're knocking it out of the park – or at least making it to first base without tripping over our own feet.

But here's a little secret: most of the game isn't won by show boaters; it's won by the steady Eddies, the ones who consistently get on base with singles and doubles.

In business, it's pretty much the same deal. Sure, we all dream of that one big deal then we buy our yacht and use hundred-dollar bills as coasters. But the reality? Success is usually built on a series of smaller wins. It's about consistently delivering, meeting deadlines, satisfying customers, and slowly but surely moving your business forward.

The Problem with the "Home Run" Mentality

Grand slams evoke memories of legendary sluggers like Babe Ruth and Hank Aaron and continues to thrill fans through the exploits of modern-day power hitters such as Aaron Judge, Rhys Hoskins, and Bryan Reynolds.

The business world boasts its own roster of grand slam hitters, from tech titans like Bill Gates, Steve Jobs, and Elon Musk, to historical game-changers such as Coco Chanel, Walt Disney, Thomas Edison, Henry Ford, and John D. Rockefeller. These visionaries didn't just succeed; they revolutionized entire industries with their unwavering dedication and brilliant ideas. Their stories of overcoming obstacles and seizing opportunities have set the benchmark for business success.

In recent times, this legacy of transformative success has expanded to diverse fields. Cultural icons like Taylor Swift, Beyoncé, and Oprah Winfrey have redefined entertainment and media, while figures like Serena Williams have become legends beyond their primary arenas. Canada too has produced its share of business grand slam hitters, including Ted Rogers in communications, Chip Wilson with Lululemon, and Tobias Lütke empowering entrepreneurs through Shopify. These success stories continue to inspire and shape the landscape of business and innovation.

While these stories are captivating and inspiring, it's important to recognize that they represent exceptional cases rather than the norm. In baseball, a grand slam needs the bases to be loaded and the right pitch at the right moment. Similarly, business grand slams require a perfect confluence and alignment of skill, timing, innovation, and often a bit of luck. Gates needed the personal computer revolution, Bezos the rise of the internet, Jobs the digital lifestyle shift, and Musk the growing concern for sustainable energy.

Singles and Doubles Players

For every Babe Ruth, whose batting average was an impressive .342, there are countless players who build their careers on singles and doubles. The highest batting average in Major League Baseball (MLB) history is held by Ty Cobb (.366), who was known for his exceptional ability to get on base consistently, not for his grand slams.

In business, we have our own version of these singles and doubles hitters. They're the unsung heroes who build solid, steady companies or careers that provide value year after year. These are the small to medium business owners, the regional managers, and the steady executives who may not make headlines, but whose consistent performance keeps the economy humming.

In my own journey, a lot of the people I have met along the way have taken diverse paths to their success. We're talking everything from auto parts distribution moguls to janitorial service tycoons and real estate titans. More on all of this in future chapters.

What strikes me most isn't the glamour of their industries (let's face it, there's nothing particularly glamorous about a business that sells auto parts, except maybe the valuation that the business was sold for), but rather their unwavering commitment to steady, reliable work. These are the folks who show up day after day, consistently delivering value, much like those baseball players who reliably get on base game after game.

Bridging the Gap: The Power of Singles and Doubles in a World of Grand Slams

While we are advocating for the unsung heroes of success, the singles and doubles hitters, let's face it: we can't ignore the allure of those grand slam moments that make headlines. So, how do we reconcile celebrating the likes of Bill Gates, Steve Jobs, Elon Musk, Taylor Swift, Oprah Winfrey, and others while championing the everyday achiever who produces exceptional results over time?

The beauty of focusing on singles and doubles is that they're achievable. They're the building blocks of confidence, the fuel for motivation, and the stepping stones to bigger goals. They're the difference between dreaming about success and getting there.

But celebrating these smaller wins doesn't mean we're settling for less. Far from it. We're playing the long game, building a career and a life that can weather any storm.

Bottom of the 1st

In the end, The Consistency Effect isn't about leaning in for a grand slam and taking a single instead. It's about understanding that those headline-grabbing successes are built on a foundation of smaller, consistent wins. It's about recognizing that by focusing on what's within our reach today, we're setting ourselves up for bigger wins tomorrow.

Key Takeaways:

1. The Singles and Doubles Approach

- Consistent performance creates more sustainable success than occasional brilliance

- Small, steady achievements compound over time into significant progress

- Reliability and dependability often matter more than sporadic brilliance

- Daily excellence creates the foundation for long-term achievement

- Patient progression builds careers that withstand changing conditions

2. Success Development Process

- Business breakthroughs typically require specific conditions that can't be manufactured at will

- Sustainable growth depends on regular, incremental improvements

- Confidence and momentum build through celebrating achievable milestones

- Mental preparation is as important as technical execution in achieving consistent results

3. Balancing Success Factors

- Strategic foundations make larger achievements possible over time

- Internal drive must be complemented by external support systems

- Ambition and patience need to be balanced for sustainable success

4. The Power of Consistency

- Small wins serve as building blocks for confidence and motivation

- Daily habits ultimately determine long-term outcomes

- Organizational backbones are built on reliable performance

- Everyday excellence deserves recognition alongside breakthrough moments

- Weathering storms becomes possible through consistent preparation

5. Growth and Development

- Big successes often rest on foundations of smaller achievements

- Perfect conditions are rare, making consistent performance more valuable

- Professional development follows predictable stages of competency building

- Learning and adaptation are ongoing processes throughout careers

- The path to greatness lies through consistent improvement rather than occasional brilliance

2nd Inning

Singles and Doubles as an Individual and in the Business

"Success is neither magical nor mysterious. Success is the natural consequence of consistently applying basic fundamentals" — Jim Rohn

---

How do you Define a Single or Double in Business and in Life?

While I often describe my business success as hitting singles and doubles. What does that really mean? Perhaps one way to start is to define a grand slam and work backwards to use the other field achievements in baseball to define various levels of business success.

Now I recognize that defining success in business is akin to describing the taste of water – it's universally experienced yet uniquely personal. Nevertheless, for the sake of our discussion, let's attempt to quantify business success, fully aware that we're treading the fine line between insightful analysis and pure abstraction.

In the major league of commerce, a "grand slam" might look something like this: a start-up experiences growth so exponential it makes Moore's Law look conservative. This start-up not only disrupts an industry but reshapes the very fabric of society. We're talking wealth in the $100 million plus range, the kind of money that doesn't just talk; it gives a full TED Talk.

A "home run" in this game might be when you've built and sold a company for somewhere between $10 to $100 million. It's the type of success that ensures your descendants will be arguing over your estate with the drama of the actors from the HBO hit series Succession.

But let's turn our gaze to the unsung heroes – the singles and doubles hitters. These are the entrepreneurs and business leaders who may not be featured in business school case studies, but whose success is no less real. A "single" might see you rounding first base with less than $1 to 3 million, while a "double" has you sliding into second with $3 to $5 million. Reach third, and you're looking at $5 to $10 million. Not exactly chump change, unless you're comparing yourself to Elon Musk, but why would you do that to yourself?

Let's be clear: these financial guideposts shouldn't be viewed as scientifically rigorous measures. They're meant to provide a general framework for discussion, not absolute definitions of success. These figures are intended to be illustrative rather than definitive. They offer a starting point for considering different levels of business achievement, but it's crucial to understand that real-world success is far more nuanced and varied.

What do Singles and Doubles Look Like in Business and in Life?

In business, success can be measured through consistent, incremental achievements. These include steady revenue growth, strong customer relationships, operational efficiency, employee development and retention, continuous product improvements, strategic partnerships, and sustainable financial practices.

Personal success, while more subjective, can also be viewed through a similar lens. It encompasses various life areas such as education, health and fitness, relationships, personal finance, career development, personal growth, travel and experiences, creativity, community involvement, and work-life balance. In each of these areas, individuals can achieve "singles" (smaller, more immediate goals) and "doubles" (larger, more significant accomplishments). For instance, in education, completing a certificate program might be a single, while earning a degree could be considered a double.

Ultimately, personal success is about the journey rather than the destination. Unlike in business, personal achievements often defy simple quantification and are more about overall life satisfaction and happiness. The key is to define your own measures of success, reflect on your goals, and have the courage to pursue them, even when they don't align with societal expectations. By acknowledging and celebrating both small and large personal milestones, individuals can construct a rich, meaningful life, one achievement at a time.

The Art of Energy Management: Knowing Your Play

In baseball, players don't swing for the fences on every pitch; a savvy businessperson knows how to allocate their efforts effectively. When you step up to the plate in your professional life, it's crucial to know the play you desire and calibrate your energy accordingly.

Consider this: if you're expending all your energy for a grand slam and only manage a bunt, there's a great deal of wasted effort – like infielders scrambling for a ball that barely leaves home plate. I've observed colleagues overplaying their hand and overspending resources on relatively insignificant events or projects. This approach not only depletes energy but can also lead to burnout and missed opportunities elsewhere. The key is to assess each situation and determine the appropriate level of input. If you're aiming for a single, put in single-level effort. If you achieve more, fantastic! But don't exhaust all your mojo on every play.

In baseball and business, it's not just about the current at-bat; it's about maintaining your stamina for a full nine innings, or in our case, a long and successful career. By mastering this art of energy management, you'll find yourself more consistently effective and better prepared for those moments when a grand slam is truly within reach.

Bottom of the 2nd

Life isn't just about swinging for the fences. The path to sustainable success – in both business and personal life – comes through understanding and valuing the power of consistent, incremental achievements. Whether it's building a business to a million-dollar milestone or completing a professional certification, these "singles and doubles" form the foundation of lasting accomplishment.

Most importantly, success requires strategic energy management: knowing when to push for breakthrough moments and when to focus on steady progress. By redefining success as a series of deliberate, well-executed smaller wins rather than occasional spectacular achievements, we create a more sustainable and fulfilling journey. Remember, it's the consistent, strategic accumulation of achievements that builds lasting success.

Key Takeaways:

1. Defining Success Milestones

- Personalized metrics matter more than universal definitions of achievement

- Financial guideposts help frame different levels of success while recognizing individual variation

- Balanced accomplishment across multiple life domains creates richer fulfillment than single-domain focus

- Incremental achievements in business and personal life follow similar patterns of development

- Journey appreciation often matters more than destination attainment

2. Strategic Energy Management

- Appropriate effort allocation prevents burnout and maximizes effectiveness

- Calibrated investment matches energy expenditure to expected returns

- Career stamina requires pacing yourself across multiple challenges

- Selective intensity preserves resources for truly important opportunities

- Situational awareness helps determine when to push and when to maintain steady effort

3. Holistic Success Framework

- Multiple life domains contribute to overall fulfillment and satisfaction

- Business and personal achievement follow similar patterns despite different metrics

- Incremental progress applies equally to financial goals and personal development

- Self-defined standards matter more than external expectations or comparisons

- Consistent accumulation of small wins creates sustainable life satisfaction

3rd Inning

Striving for Excellence:
The Path to Achieving a GRAND SLAM

"Yesterday's home runs don't win today's games, but they teach you what's possible." — Babe Ruth

---

Learning Objectives:

After reading this chapter, you will:

- Understand and apply the GRAND SLAM framework for success

- Recognize how different success elements work together synergistically

- Learn to balance humility and confidence in achieving success

- Master the Four Stages of Competence in skill development

- Understand how consistent effort leads to extraordinary achievement

- Learn to develop and nurture each element of the GRAND SLAM model

- Appreciate the role of persistence and practice in mastering skills

GRAND SLAM: Decoding Success, One Letter at a Time

As I reflected on the elements that contribute to remarkable achievements or the lack thereof, I found myself playing with the idea of GRAND SLAM as an acronym. Now, I know what you're thinking – "Oh great, another guy forcing concepts into a catchy acronym."

I'll be the first to admit that squeezing ideas into an acronym can sometimes feel like picking players just because their names spell something clever. But I believe GRAND SLAM is different. These elements made the team because I believe each component has a significant effect on the outcome, not because they fit a predetermined roster. What follows is my attempt to break down the components of success. It's not a magic formula, and it certainly doesn't guarantee you'll hit a home run every time. But I hope that by sharing these thoughts, we might all gain some insights into how we can improve our game.

GRAND SLAM

G – Great Idea R – Resilience A – Ambition N – Network D – Discipline	S – Skill L – Luck A – Action M – Mentors

GRAND SLAM: A Deeper Dive

Great Idea: Seeds of Grand Slams

"All our dreams can come true if we have the courage to pursue them." — Walt Disney

First up let's talk about great ideas, those sparks of inspiration that have the potential to change the game entirely. There's no denying it: a truly great idea is often the cornerstone of a business grand slam. But not every world-changing idea announces itself with fireworks and fanfare.

Think about it. Some of the most revolutionary business concepts started out looking, well, pretty ordinary. Take Amazon, for instance. Jeff Bezos didn't set out to create the "everything store" or dominate cloud computing. Nope, he started with a simple notion: selling books online. It was a solid single, maybe a double in baseball terms. But through discipline, adaptability, and a keen eye for opportunity, that modest online bookstore transformed into an e-commerce empire and a leader in web services.

Or consider Netflix. Did you know they initially mailed out VHS tapes? It's a far cry from the streaming giant they are today. But that initial idea – making movie rentals more convenient – contained the seed of something much bigger.

The lesson here? Great ideas don't always wear flashy uniforms. Sometimes, they show up in work boots, ready to put in the hours. It's not about having a fully formed, industry-disrupting concept right out of the gate. It's about starting with a solid premise and being willing to nurture it, adapt it, and sometimes completely reinvent it as you go.

This is where discipline and resilience come into play. A great idea without taking the action to see it through is like a powerful swing that misses the ball. It might look impressive, but it won't get you on base.

So, while we celebrate the great ideas that seem to change the world overnight, let's not forget the power of ideas that grow over time. Today's modest concept could be tomorrow's game-changer.

"A dream doesn't become reality through magic; it takes sweat, determination and hard work." Colin Powell.

Resilience: The Comeback Kid of Business

"Failure comes when you stay where you have fallen." Socrates

Let's talk about resilience. It's not just a fancy buzzword; it's the gritty, no-quit attitude that separates the major leaguers from the benchwarmers in the big game of business.

Think of resilience as your business's immune system. Just like your body fights off germs and bounces back from illness, resilience helps your business weather storms, adapt to curveballs, and come back stronger after every setback.

In baseball, even the greatest sluggers strike out. Babe Ruth, the Sultan of Swat himself, struck out 1,330 times. But you know what? He also hit 714 home runs. That's resilience in action. It's the same in business. Steve Jobs got booted from Apple, the company he founded. But did he curl up in a ball and call it quits? Heck no! After leaving

Apple in 1985, Jobs didn't just sit around licking his wounds. He went on to found NeXT Computer, a company that developed high-end computers for the education sector. While NeXT wasn't a runaway success, it became the foundation for many of the ideas that would later revolutionize Apple.

That's not all. During this time, Jobs also acquired a little computer graphics division from Lucasfilm. You might have heard of it – a little outfit called Pixar. Under Jobs' guidance, Pixar went on to create ground-breaking animated films and eventually sold to Disney for $7.4 billion. Talk about a comeback!

When Jobs returned to Apple in 1997, he brought with him the experience, skills, and technologies he'd developed during his time away. He led Apple from the brink of bankruptcy to become one of the most valuable companies on the planet. This journey wasn't just a return; it was a reinvention, both of Jobs himself and of Apple.

Jobs' story is a masterclass in resilience. He took his setbacks and turned them into stepping stones, using each challenge as an opportunity to learn, grow, and ultimately come back stronger. He came back and led Apple to become one of the most valuable companies on the planet.

But here's the real magic of resilience – it's not just about you. It's about inspiring your team to keep pushing forward, even when it feels like you're down to your last out. It's about maintaining a positive outlook that's more infectious than a yawn in a boring meeting. When your team sees you bouncing back from setbacks with a smile and a plan, they'll be ready to charge into battle with you, no matter the odds.

Resilience isn't about never falling. It's about how quickly you get back up, how you learn from the fall, and how you use that experience to move even higher next time. It's the quality that turns today's strikeout into tomorrow's grand slam. So cultivate it, cherish it, and watch as it transforms your business from a rookie prospect into a hall of fame contender. Falling down is not a failure.

Ambition: The Rocket Fuel of Success

"Only those who will risk going too far can possibly find out how far one can go." — T. S. Eliot

Let's talk about ambition, the fire in your belly that turns "what if" into "what's next." It's not just about dreaming big; it's about dreaming big and then chasing those dreams.

Ambition is your inner Babe Ruth, pointing to the stands and calling your shot. It's about setting goals that make your palms sweat and your heart race.

But here's the thing – ambition isn't just about setting those lofty goals. It's about having the drive to achieve them. It's about pushing yourself beyond your comfort zone. It's about looking at your current success and saying, "That's great, but what if we could do more?"

Think about Jeff Bezos. He didn't stop at creating an online bookstore. His ambition pushed him to create "the everything store," and then to revolutionize cloud computing with AWS. That's ambition in action, always reaching for the next level, always asking, "What's the next pitch we can knock out of the park?"

Ambition is what gets you out of bed at 5 AM to work on your business plan. It's what keeps you going when everyone else says it can't be done. It's the voice in your head that says, "One more try, one more pitch, one more swing." It's the unwavering passion that turns a small start-up in a garage into a global tech giant.

But let's be clear – ambition isn't about blind optimism. It's about coupling those big dreams with hard work and smart strategies. It's about being willing to put in the hours, to face the setbacks, to learn from the strikeouts, all in pursuit of that grand slam moment.

Network: Your All-Star Team in the Big Leagues of Business

Think of networking like building your fantasy team. You're not just picking random players; you're strategically assembling a diverse roster of all-stars who can help you win in any situation. Your network is your power hitter when you need to close a big deal, your relief pitcher for when you're in a tight spot, and your scout alerting you to the next big opportunity.

But a great network isn't built overnight. It takes time, practice, and a whole lot of persistence. You're not just collecting contacts; you're cultivating relationships. It's about giving as much as you get, cheering from the sidelines when your connections hit their home runs, and being there to offer support when they strike out.

Your network is your eyes and ears on the ground, keeping you informed about industry trends, potential opportunities, and looming challenges. It's your brain trust, offering insights and advice when you're facing a tough decision.

In business, no one makes it to the hall of fame alone. Your network is the team that will introduce you to your next big client, mentor you through a career change, or partner with you on a game-changing venture.

So, get out there and start building your all-star team. Attend those industry events like they're spring training. Reach out to that person you admire as if you're scouting the next big talent. Offer help and support to others like you're the team captain. Because in the end, your network isn't just about who you know – it's about who's on your side, ready to step up when you need them.

Building Your All-Star Network: A Playbook

Because building a powerful network is such a crucial component of success, lets breakdown the concept further:

Diversity is Key:

Just like a baseball team needs a mix of power hitters, speedsters, and defensive specialists, your network should be diverse.

Look for people with different:

- Skills: Technical experts, creative thinkers, strategic planners.

- Experiences: Industry veterans, fresh-faced innovators, career-switchers.

- Backgrounds: Various industries, cultures, and perspectives.

Complement Your Strengths and Weaknesses:

- If you're a big-picture thinker, connect with detail-oriented individuals.

- Are you a tech whiz? Seek out those with strong people skills.

- Analytical mind? Find some creative types to balance you out.

Seek Specific Expertise:

- Industry Insiders: Those with deep knowledge of your field.

- Cross-Industry Experts: They can offer fresh perspectives.

- Functional Specialists: Finance gurus, marketing mavens, HR wizards.

Look for Connectors:

- These are the social butterflies who seem to know everyone.

- They can exponentially expand your reach.

Mentors and Coaches:

- Seek those who've "been there, done that" in your field.

- Look for individuals who challenge and inspire you.

Peer Support:

- Connect with others at your level for mutual support and idea-sharing. Up-and-Comers:

- Don't overlook young talent; they often bring fresh perspectives and energy.

Value Alignment:

- Seek individuals who share your core values and ethics.

Remember, building a network isn't about collecting the most business cards or LinkedIn connections. It's about fostering genuine relationships. Here's how to do it:

- Be Authentic: Don't just reach out when you need something

- Give Before You Take: Offer help, share insights, make introductions

- Stay in Touch: Regular, meaningful interactions keep relationships strong

- Be Curious: Ask questions, show genuine interest in others

- Follow Up: After meetings or events, reach out to continue the conversation

- Meet People: Not virtually; actually meet people.

Building a powerful network takes time and effort, but it's an investment that pays dividends throughout your career. Just like a baseball team practices daily, make networking a consistent part of your routine. You never know when that connection you made at last year's conference might throw you the perfect pitch for your next big opportunity.

Discipline: The Backbone of Your Success Story

"The main thing is to keep the main thing the main thing." Stephen R. Covey, an American author, The 7 Habits of Highly Effective People.

Discipline is your daily commitment to excellence, the unsexy hero of your success story. It's not about occasional bursts of motivation; it's about showing up every single day, rain or shine, ready to put in the work.

Discipline is what keeps you going when motivation fades, and the initial excitement of a new project wears off. It's the voice in your head that says, "One more rep, one more call, one more hour." It's the foundation that supports your ambition, the fuel that powers your resilience, and the structure that maximizes your network.

Steve Jobs once said, "Half of success is perseverance." The ability to effectively implement plans and strategies often makes the difference between success and failure. It's not enough to have a brilliant idea or a solid business plan. The real magic happens in the execution: the timely product releases, the high-quality customer service, the continuous improvements that drive growth.

But let's be honest, discipline isn't always glamorous. In fact, it often feels like drudgery. Yet, as the saying goes, "We get things done through the miracle of drudgery." It's those small, daily efforts that accumulate over time, building into significant results that can transform your business and your life.

Championships aren't won on game day alone. They're won in the countless hours of preparation beforehand.

Because here's the thing about success, it's not always the most talented who win. More often, it's those who show up every day, ready to put in the work, regardless of how they feel. That's the power of discipline. That's how you turn singles and doubles into a winning season.

Skill: Your Secret Weapon in the Big Leagues

Skill is not just about being born with a golden arm. It's about taking whatever natural talents you've got and turning them into your secret weapon through ambition, resilience, and a whole lot of practice (discipline).

Think of skill as your Swiss Army knife in the unpredictable game of business. It's not just about what you can do right now; it's about what you're willing to learn, adapt, and master as the game evolves. It's about having the eye to spot a game-changing opportunity and the chops to knock it out of the park when it comes your way.

But skill isn't just about what you can do; it's about when you do it. It's about having the business acumen to recognize when the market is primed for your product, and the ability to swing for the fences at just the right moment.

Think about it. Steve Jobs didn't just create great products; he had an uncanny ability to introduce them at precisely the right moment, when the market was ready for a revolution. That's skill in action – the perfect blend of ability and timing.

Skill is what turns a good idea into a game-changing innovation. It's what transforms a struggling start-up into a market leader.

But let's dive deeper into what it really means to hone your skills. It's not just about the highlight reels or game day performances. The real work happens behind the scenes, in ways that might surprise you. In business, this might mean practicing your pitch until you can deliver it in your sleep or running through financial scenarios until the numbers dance in your dreams.

But skill development isn't just physical – there's a crucial mental component that often goes overlooked. Elite athletes spend as much time training their minds as they do their bodies. They practice visualization techniques, running the bases in their minds or mentally rehearsing their swings. They work on getting still, finding that perfect state of focus where the noise of the crowd fades away and all that's left is the ball and the bat.

This mental prep is about leaving the mind uncluttered and ready to seize the day – or as the Romans would say, "Carpe Diem!" It's about being so prepared, so in tune with your skills, that when opportunity knocks, you can react without hesitation.

It's about building such a solid foundation of knowledge and practice that when your moment comes, you can step up to the plate with the quiet confidence of a seasoned pro.

In the end, it's not just about having skills - it's about having skills so ingrained, so second-nature, that when opportunity throws you a curveball, you'll be ready to knock it out of the park.

Luck: The Wild Card in Your Winning Hand

"Life is full of surprises and serendipity. Being open to unexpected turns in the road is an important part of success. If you try to plan every step, you may miss those wonderful twists and turns." Condoleezza Rice, former U.S. Secretary of State

Ok luck - that elusive, unpredictable factor that can turn a solid single into a game-winning grand slam. But here's the thing about luck in business: it's not just about four-leaf clovers and rabbits' feet. It's about being ready to catch it when it comes your way.

But luck isn't just serendipity. Remember what the great Walt Disney said? "This business is all about luck, but it's amazing how much luckier the person who works 50 hours a week is than the person who works 40 hours a week." Ain't that the truth? The harder you work, the luckier you get.

Luck is also more than hard work; it's about smart work. It's about having your head in the game, your eyes wide open, ready to spot that golden opportunity when it presents itself. It's about being in the right place at the right time – and knowing what to do when you get there.

Consider Jensen Huang founding NVIDIA. Sure, he was lucky to start the company just as PC gaming was gaining momentum. But his true genius wasn't just in seeing the potential of graphics processors; it was in repeatedly reimagining their purpose. From gaming to scientific computing to AI, Huang transformed NVIDIA's GPUs from specialized gaming chips into the engines powering the AI revolution. That's not just luck meeting preparation – it's preparation creating luck through continuous innovation and reinvention. Now, let's add another quote, this time by Dr. Phil McGraw, who said, "Winners do what losers won't." While others are sitting on the bench, waiting for their lucky break, winners are out there, putting in the extra hours, taking the risks, and creating their own opportunities.

So, how do you become one of these lucky winners? It's simple, but it ain't easy. It's about showing up every day, ready to play. It's about keeping your eyes peeled for opportunities, no matter how small. It's about being willing to take that risk, make that call, or try that new strategy when others are playing it safe.

Remember, in the game of business, luck favors the prepared. It favors the bold. It favors those who are willing to step up to the plate, even when the odds are stacked against them. Because you can't control luck, but you can sure as heck control how ready you are when it comes knocking.

Action: The Courage to Step Up to the Plate and Swing

"I'd rather be fired for what I did than for what I didn't do." Jack Welch, the former CEO of General Electric

Action is the spark that turns potential into reality. It's the difference between dreaming about success and achieving it. Action is seizing opportunities, making decisive moves, and having the courage to step up when the stakes are high. It's not about being busy; it's about being bold. It's the difference between having a great idea and bringing that idea to life.

Action is about having the guts to step out of the dugout and onto the field. It's about taking that first step, making that first call, sending that first email. It's about turning your business plan from a document gathering dust on your desk into a living, breathing enterprise. Let's face it, everyone who has had a shower has had a good idea. It is the person who dries themselves off and goes out and turns that idea into a game-changing product. It's what transforms a struggling start-up into a market leader.

But here's the key – action isn't reckless. It's calculated risk-taking, informed by your skill, experience, discipline, and ambition. It's about knowing when to swing and when to hold back, when to go all-in and when to play it safe. It is about listening to your mentors and taking their advice when it seems right.

Mentors: Your All-Star Coaches in the Game of Success

"You can observe a lot by just watching." Yogi Berra

Mentors are not your grandfather's wise old sages stroking their beards and spouting fortune cookie wisdom. No, they're your personal dream team of coaches, ready to help you turn your raw talent into hall of fame material.

But the best mentors are not just there to pat you on the back and tell you you're doing great. A great mentor is like a tough-love coach who'll call you out when you're slacking and push you to swing harder when you're playing it safe. They're the ones who'll spot the flaw in your strategy or approach before it costs you the game.

But mentorship isn't about being a fan in the bleachers. It's not about sitting back and waiting for wisdom to be bestowed upon you. It's about actively seeking out those relationships, showing up ready to learn, and being willing to put their advice into action. And the absolute most important thing is it is about being coachable by embracing feedback, showing a willingness to change, maintaining humility, seeking proactive learning, applying consistency, and engaging in reflective practice.

Great mentors don't just teach you; they show you how to inspire your team, how to bounce back from a crushing defeat, how to lead with integrity. They help you understand that every interaction, every decision, every emotional response ripples out and affects your entire team. That's the kind of wisdom that turns good players into great leaders.

So how do you make the most of mentorship? It's simple:

1. Be hungry for knowledge. Come to every interaction with your mentor ready to learn.

2. Be humble. Check your ego at the door and be open to criticism and new ideas.

3. Be proactive. Don't wait for mentors to come to you – seek them out.

4. Be grateful. Show appreciation for your mentor's time and wisdom.

5. Be a mentor yourself. As you grow, start sharing your own knowledge with others.

In the end, mentorship is about more than just personal success. It's about creating a legacy, about passing on knowledge, about leaving the game better than you found it. So, seek out those mentors, soak up their wisdom, and then pay it forward. Because in the grand game of life and business, the true champions aren't just the ones with the biggest trophies. They're the ones who help others win too.

Perceptions of Success – Balancing Dumb Luck with the Midas Touch

The delicate balance between humility and confidence in the face of success presents a psychological high-wire act worthy of Cirque du Soleil, albeit one performed in the theater of the mind rather than under the big top. On one end of the wire, we find the excessively modest, those who might attribute their Nobel Prize-winning research to a fortuitous alignment of stars rather than years of rigorous work.

While such humility can be refreshing, by consistently underplaying their accomplishments, these self-proclaimed lucky people may dramatically understate their expertise and hard-won insights.

On the opposite end of the spectrum, we find those who indulge in excessive self-confidence, verging on arrogance. They equate previous success with innate skill. This "Midas Touch" mindset, while inspiring, carries serious risks. It often leads to dangerous overconfidence, blinding people to the complexities and unpredictability involved in sustaining success. I've seen this firsthand in the corporate world – executives who think their early victories mean they'll always succeed, only to be left stunned when future ventures fall short.

The Midas Touch mentality is especially risky in the ever-changing business landscape, where what worked in the past can quickly become outdated. It's crucial to strike a balance between confidence in one's skills and an understanding of the need to adapt, stay aware of external factors, and continually improve.

Ultimately, the most successful individuals often demonstrate a remarkable ability to hold two seemingly contradictory ideas in tension: pride in their accomplishments and humility in the face of fortune's role in their success.

Fortune may favor the bold, but it also has a wicked sense of humor. The moment you think you've mastered the game is often when it decides to change all the rules and replace the chessboard with a Rubik's cube. Stay humble, stay hungry, and for heaven's sake, don't let that golden touch convince you that you can turn lead into gold.

To obtain a summary download of the Grand Slam Framework please visit www.consistency-edge.com/pages/shop.

Conscious Champions: Illuminating the Path from Lucky Breaks to Legendary Performance

"Until you make the unconscious conscious, it will direct your life and you will call it fate." Karl Jung

In this section I would like to use a framework called the Four Stages of Competency to add to our GRAND SLAM elements to further examine why some individuals ascribe their success to mere chance while others define it as natural talent. The "Four Stages of Competence" framework was first described by DePhillips, Berliner, and Cribbin in their 1960 playbook, "Management of Training Programs," and later popularized by Noel Burch.

The Four Stages of Competency:

1. **Unconscious Incompetence:** The individual is unaware of their lack of skill and doesn't recognize the value of learning it.

2. **Conscious Incompetence:** The person becomes aware of their skill deficiency and recognizes the importance of learning, though they still struggle.

3. **Conscious Competence:** The individual can perform the skill but needs to concentrate deliberately on each step.

4. **Unconscious Competence:** The skill becomes second nature, allowing the person to perform it effortlessly and automatically without conscious thought.

The Four Stages of Competence framework, when applied to the GRAND SLAM model, offers a powerful roadmap for personal and professional growth that can transform your approach to success. Here's how I use it:

By breaking down the path to success into clear stages, the two concepts together show that excellence isn't just for the naturally gifted. Anyone can progress from clueless rookie to seasoned pro with the right mindset and effort.

It promotes self-awareness. Understanding where you are in this framework allows you to accurately assess your skills and identify areas for improvement. This self-knowledge is crucial for targeted growth.

It encourages perseverance. Recognizing that feeling incompetent is a natural part of the learning process can help you push through frustration and self-doubt. It's not about being perfect from the start; it's about consistent progress.

It validates the importance of deliberate practice. The framework highlights that mastery comes from conscious effort and repetition, reinforcing the value of the "singles and doubles" approach to success.

It offers a blueprint for coaching and mentorship. Whether you're a leader developing your team or an individual seeking guidance, this framework provides a clear structure for identifying needs and measuring progress.

It aligns perfectly with the GRAND SLAM model, showing how each element can be developed and internalized over time. This integration provides a comprehensive approach to achieving and sustaining success.

It emphasizes the long-term nature of true success. By illustrating the progression from unconscious incompetence to unconscious competence, it reinforces that sustainable achievement is a journey, not a single event.

In essence, this framework doesn't just describe the stages of learning; it provides a powerful tool for intentional growth. It reminds us that mastery in any field – be it business, sports, or life – is attainable through awareness, effort, and persistence. By understanding and applying this concept, you can transform your approach to challenges, accelerate your learning, and ultimately achieve the kind of effortless excellence that defines true success.

Legend in the Making: Redefining Consistency and Excellence

Before we wrap up this inning, let's talk about a player who's rewriting the rulebook on consistency and skill, Shohei Ohtani. If you're not a baseball fan, you might be wondering, "Who's this Ohtani guy, and why should I care?" It is because Ohtani's story is a tremendous example of the Consistency Effect in action.

Shohei Ohtani isn't just playing the game; he's changing it. He's what fans call a two-way player, excelling both as a pitcher and a hitter. Now, in baseball terms, that's like being a master chef who's also a world-class sommelier. It just doesn't happen. Except, with Ohtani, it does.

Ohtani didn't just wake up one day and decide to dominate both sides of the game. His success is the result of years of consistent, persistent effort. It's the embodiment of the singles and doubles approach we've been talking about. From his early days in Japan to his current stardom in Major League Baseball, Ohtani has been hitting those singles and doubles day in and day out. He's been in the batting cage, perfecting his swing. He's been on the mound, honing his pitches. He's been in the gym, building the strength and stamina to excel in both roles. Every day, every practice, every game – it's all been about consistent improvement.

And the results? Well, they're nothing short of spectacular. Ohtani isn't just good at both pitching and hitting; he's great at both. He's breaking records, winning awards, and leaving fans and fellow players alike in awe. He's not just playing the game; he's redefining what's possible in baseball, and we might just be witnessing the rise of the greatest baseball player of all time.

In the game of business and life, we might not all be Ohtanis. But we can all learn from his approach. We can all strive for that level of consistency, that commitment to excellence in everything we do. Because who knows? With enough singles and doubles, enough small wins and steady progress, we might just find ourselves changing the game in our own fields.

Remember, the path to greatness isn't a sprint; it's a marathon. It's about showing up every day, ready to swing, ready to pitch, ready to give it your all. That's the Consistency Effect in action. That's the Ohtani way. And that, folks, is how you become a legend in whatever game you're playing.

Bottom of the 3rd Inning

And what a long inning it was. In summary, it is understanding and mastering how your Great Idea provides direction, Resilience keeps you going, Ambition drives you forward, your Network supports you, Discipline builds your foundation, Skill sharpens your abilities, Luck provides opportunities, Action makes things happen, and Mentors guide you along the way. All of these elements are reinforced by the Four Stages of Competence, providing a structured approach to achieving and sustaining success in business and life. By recognizing the multifaceted nature of success and thinking about it more consciously, individuals can develop more significant and sustained achievements.

Key Takeaways:

The GRAND SLAM Framework

1. **Great Ideas need nurturing and development over time**

   • Resilience enables recovery and growth from setbacks

   • Ambition drives continuous improvement and vision

   • Network provides crucial support and opportunities

   • Discipline ensures consistent execution

   • Skill requires continuous development and practice

   • Luck favours the prepared and persistent

   • Action transforms ideas into reality

   • Mentors guide and accelerate growth

2. Success Development Process

- Excellence comes from consistent, daily effort

- Great achievements often start as modest ideas

- Success requires both internal drive and external support

- The journey to mastery follows predictable stages

- Mental preparation is as important as skill development

3. Balancing Success Factors

- Balance humility with confidence

- Combine preparation with opportunity

- Mix strategic thinking with decisive action

- Blend personal effort with mentor guidance

- Balance ambitious goals with realistic execution

4. The Power of Consistency

- Success is built through daily habits and practices

- Small wins compound into significant achievements

- Excellence requires both physical and mental preparation

- Consistent effort leads to breakthrough moments

- The Ohtani example shows how consistency creates excellence

5. Growth and Development

- Success is a journey through distinct competency stages

- Mastery requires conscious effort before becoming natural

- Learning and development are ongoing processes

- Excellence requires both technical and mental skills

- The path to greatness is through consistent improvement

4th Inning

Striking Out: A Lesson in Resilience and the GRAND SLAM Effect

---

"Our greatest glory is not in never falling, but in rising every time we fall."— Confucius

---

Learning Objectives:

After reading this chapter, you will:

- Understand how failure can be a catalyst for future success

- Learn to identify and apply transferable skills across different domains

- Recognize the role of resilience in personal and professional growth

- Understand how to leverage the GRAND SLAM framework in challenging situations

- Learn to transform setbacks into opportunities

- Appreciate the importance of maintaining enthusiasm through failures

- Identify patterns of success and failure in your own journey

Strike 1

Let's talk about striking out and bouncing back. You see, in the business world, we often hear about the grim statistics of failure. Roughly 20% of new businesses strike out in their first year, 50% by year five, and a whopping 70% by year ten. The latter is the equivalent of maintaining a .300 batting average for a decade – no small feat, let me tell you.

But here's the thing about statistics: they don't tell the whole story. They don't capture the passion, the pivots, and the perseverance that often lead to success. Let me share a story from my own playbook that at a minimum is hopefully amusing and might just resonate with some of you.

I was born and raised in Toronto, Canada, in an upper-middle class family. Picture a seven-year-old me, signed up for guitar lessons by well-intentioned parents. There I was, fumbling through a song that had zero relevance to someone my age ("Little Brown Jug" for those who need to know.) From down the hall, I could hear the rhythmic beats of a drum kit echoing through the building. It was love at first listen. But like many great love stories, this one had its share of obstacles.

First, despite my self-professed yet unrealized passion for playing drums, my parents said no. We lived in an apartment and there is no way that that would have worked out.

Junior high rolled around, and a musical aptitude test (whoever thought that was a good idea?) landed me in the string class. There I was, sawing away at a violin (definitely against my will), watching the percussionists through a sound-proof glass window between the band rooms. There they were having all the fun next door and doing what I wanted to do. Love denied. Talk about being so close, yet so far.

It wasn't until my family moved when I was 15 that I finally got my shot. "What do you want to play?" the music teacher of my new junior high asked. "Drums," I said, without missing a beat. He pointed me to the bass drum, a starting position if there ever was one. But hey, I was in the game!

Now, here's where our story takes an interesting turn. After months of dedication, countless hours of practice, and more than a few blisters, I finally worked my way up from the lowly bass drum to the coveted snare drum. But I didn't stop there. No sir, I had my sights set on the crown jewel of the percussion section – the full drum set.

The day I finally sat behind that complete kit; I felt like a king on his throne. The cymbals gleamed like polished gold, the toms stood proud like loyal subjects, and the bass drum... well, it was an old friend by now. This was my moment of triumph, my time to shine.

But just as I was basking in the glow of this mini-success, ready to unleash my newfound skills on the world, that high school teacher – you remember him, right? The one who gave me my first drum break? He drops a bombshell that could've shattered lesser dreams.

"You're a good drummer but you'll never be a great drummer," he said, his words as flat and uninspiring as a poorly tuned snare drum.

Now, let me tell you something about naysayers. They're like the umpires who make bad calls, infuriating in the moment, but often the very thing that ignites a fire in your belly.

His doubt? It didn't crush me. Oh no. It lit a fire under me. In that moment, with his words still ringing in my ears, I made a silent vow. I wasn't just going to prove him wrong; I was going to prove him very wrong, one beat at a time.

So, I gripped those sticks tighter, set my jaw, and prepared to practice like my life depended on it – two, sometimes three hours a day. My poor mother's China cabinet rattled like it was caught in an earthquake. I devoured albums, dissecting the techniques of the greats. I signed up for lessons, determined to be a great drummer.

Driven by my passion for the instrument, my love for rock music, and a little bit of determination to prove my music teacher wrong, I was able to achieve a level of proficiency that I was proud of. I was able to master the techniques of my mentors, including John Bonham (Led Zeppelin), Ian Paice (Deep Purple), and ultimately Neil Peart (Rush). With my skills at an all-time high, I could smell success as a rockstar. I had the great idea, I had the skills, what else did I need?

But here's where I made a rookie mistake. In my first year of university, I let my passion for drumming overshadow everything else. I was gigging in bars until the wee hours, then sleeping through morning classes. I was going for a grand slam of fortune and fame as a rock star at the exclusions of all else. My initial academic performance? Let's just say it was a strikeout.

Convinced I was destined for rock stardom, I doubled down and dropped out of university, much to my parent's dismay. For three years, I chased that dream, dealing with the kind of ego clashes and immature emotional drama that makes a corporate boardroom battle look like a friendly game of monopoly. My dad wasn't wrong when he said the music business was more brutal than "actual" business.

After three long years of moneyless gigs and driving a taxi full time to afford a modest living, reality hit me like a curveball to the gut. While my high school buddies were building careers, buying houses, and starting families, I was still trying to make it big.

Let's break down my early strikeout using our GRAND SLAM framework. Before we dive in, I want to be clear about something: my 18-year-old self had about as much understanding of The Grand Slam concepts as a Little Leaguer had at their first big game about what it took to produce a hit – lots of energy and excitement, but not much understanding of the strike zone. It's only years later, looking back at this experience, that I've been able to see how these elements played out in my life.

Before we start, I would like to mention that while the elements of the GRAND SLAM framework can be applied to just about any situation, some are going to have more impact than others, depending on the situation. I'm not going to force every element into every story just to tick all the boxes. So, let's look at how some of these GRAND SLAM elements factored into my drumming dreams and preliminary academic strikeout:

Great Idea: My passion for drumming was the spark. I was following the adage, "Find something you like to do and get someone to pay you to do it." Becoming a Rock Star was my ticket to the big league, but I lacked a clear vision of how to turn it into a sustainable career.

Resilience: I showed plenty of this in my relentless practice. Resilience emerged time and time again as the psychodrama that is the interpersonal dynamics of youth, creativity, and ego played out. Being in a band can make even the most dysfunctional families seem normal. Looking back now, I also believe that I may have given up on my passion early because I became scared that life was passing me by.

Ambition: I had it in abundance, but it was narrowly focused on drumming at the expense of everything else.

Discipline: I had incredible discipline when it came to practicing but lacked it in other areas of my life. I was like a pitcher with a wicked fastball but no control: all power, no precision.

Skill: I was developing my drumming skills rapidly but not balancing them with other crucial life skills. I was a one-tool player in a game that required a full set.

Mentors: I want to spend a little time expanding on this element. While I had drum teachers, I lacked mentors who could guide me in circumnavigating the music industry, and others who would help me in balancing my passion with practical life considerations.

It's crucial to understand that many people in your life are models, whether you realize it or not. Some are shining examples to be emulated, like a seasoned pro showing a rookie the ropes. Others, well, they're more like cautionary tales, the "what not to do" lessons of life.

Take my high school music teacher, for instance. His initial proclamation that I wouldn't be a great drummer lit a fire under me, but it was fueled more by vengeance and spite than anything else. There is no question that this was a very strong form of passion. If I thought for one minute that his ultimate intention was to inspire me to be a better drummer, I might have sought him out later and thanked him. But the reality? He was basically just an angry man. Rather than the old saying, "Those who can't, teach," it seemed more like "Those who can't, criticize."

Looking back, it's clear that while I had some of the GRAND SLAM elements in play, they weren't working together in harmony. It was like having a team of all-star players but no game plan – lots of talent, but no direction. And when it came to mentors, I was swinging blindly, taking motivation where I could find it, even if it came from a place of negativity.

This retrospective analysis isn't about beating myself up over past mistakes. It's about understanding the game better so we can play smarter in the future. Because in the end, whether it's in music, academics, or business, success isn't just about having all the GRAND SLAM elements; it's about knowing how to use them together to create a winning strategy. And sometimes, it's about recognizing that the most valuable lessons can come from the most unexpected sources, even from those who doubt you.

Speaking about doubt, let me take you back a bit in my musical story. When I broke the news to my parents that I was dropping out of university, my father, with all the gravity of an umpire calling a game-changing play, said, "If you do this, you'll never go back to school."

Now, my dad wasn't trying to use reverse psychology on me. He was genuinely concerned, pitching what he thought was sage advice. But to my ears, it sounded like he was calling the game before I'd even stepped up to the plate. I remember at the time telling him that I was convinced that even if this music thing didn't work out, I could redirect that passion and still knock it out of the park in another field. Looking back, I'm amazed my 19-year-old self had that kind of clarity. Little did I know that this would come true.

Time for a Change-Up

Once I decided that my Rock Star ambitions were not going to work out, I had to decide what to do next. I figured that I needed to get a university degree. So, swallowing my pride (which, let me tell you, was about as easy as swallowing a baseball),

I headed back to university as a mature student. But something had changed. I approached my studies with the same manic intensity I'd given to drumming, but passion doesn't immediately translate into talent.

In my first economics class I was surrounded by a sea of 500 faces, all younger than me if you have forgotten. The professor stepped up to the plate and delivered this fastball: "Look to your right, look to your left – one of you won't be here by Christmas." Then he launched into his lecture and suddenly I'm feeling like a Little Leaguer who's wandered onto a Major League field. It might as well have been in a foreign language for all I understood. Meanwhile, my fellow students were nodding along like they've heard it all before. It felt like everyone else had gone through spring training, which I had somehow missed.

Come midterm time, I swing for the fences and end up with a minor league "C," nowhere near good enough to make it to business school. I knew I needed to step up my game, and fast.

Around the same time, I was trying to write my first 10-page essay for a history class. It was like trying to pitch a perfect game with a wiffle ball. I was downing caffeine pills and pulling all-nighters, just trying to force out those 10 pages. Again, without even handing in the paper, my self-doubt crept in and was telling me that I was again going to score an underwhelming grade, nowhere near good enough for business school.

At this point, I decided that I was not going to throw in the towel. I doubled down and started studying even harder than before. I spent hour after hour in the same basement where I practiced drums, this time reading, writing and giving myself mock tests.

Let's break down this renewed approach to academics using our GRAND SLAM framework.

Resilience: I now realize that my initial "strikeout" in university wasn't because I couldn't hit the ball. It was because I wasn't even swinging. I'd put all my chips on hitting a grand slam in the music world. This time around academics became my priority.

Ambition: My drive to succeed in university was as intense as my earlier passion for drumming. I wasn't just there to pass; I was there to excel. It fueled my resilience.

Discipline: The rigorous practice schedule I'd maintained for drumming translated perfectly into a structured study routine. I attacked my coursework with the same dedication I'd given to mastering complex rhythms.

Action: Instead of just dreaming about success, I did the work every single day. I was training for the academic equivalent of the World Series.

The Proof is in the Results

With not even a hint of modesty, I must tell you that I scored the highest final mark in my economics class and was called out by name by the professor in front of my classmates. I ended up with an "A+" in that course and all my other courses too. Oh, and that essay I thought was garbage? I turned it in and got an "A." (I really cannot believe that I've come from that place to now having written an entire book.)

It was the kind of confidence boost that fundamentally changed my perspective. From there I made the Dean's Honor Roll that year and every single year thereafter. It was like hitting a home run in every game of the season. This comeback wasn't just a single or a double; it was a home run that proved I could excel in more than one field.

This experience taught me a valuable lesson. The skills and mindset that make you successful in one arena can often translate to success in another. It's not about the specific game you're playing. It's about how you approach it. Whether you're keeping time on a drum kit or keeping up with coursework, it's your ambition, discipline, and resilience that make the difference. The disappointment and self-doubt I felt were intense, but they also fueled my determination to succeed in a new direction. Every disappointment became not an ending but a new beginning. I realize now that this experience became the cornerstone of the confidence I needed to believe that I could change careers. Little did I know how often that would come into play in my future.

The Relationship Between Success and Failure

One of my favorite Hall of Fame quotes is "Success consists of going from failure to failure without loss of enthusiasm." This quote is often mistakenly attributed to Churchill and its true origins are unknown. Nonetheless it is a great saying just the same. I may have struck out in my music career, but I used that experience to hit a home run in academics, setting me up for future success in business.

Remember, even legends like Elon Musk and Mark Zuckerberg have faced their share of adversity.

Musk faced near-bankruptcy with both Tesla and SpaceX, while Zuckerberg, of Facebook fame, incurred the wrath of investors for the seemingly unprofitable investments in the so-called metaverse. Neither of them let these failures define them. Instead, they used them as stepping stones to even greater success.

Bottom of the 4th Inning:

This chapter illustrates the transformative power of resilience and adaptability through personal experience. From a failed music career to academic excellence, this story demonstrates how the same qualities that drive success in one field can be redirected to achieve excellence in another. The journey emphasizes that failure isn't final – it's often the foundation for future success when approached with the right mindset and determination. The past does not have to dictate the future.

Key Takeaways:

1. Failure as a Foundation

- Setbacks can provide valuable lessons for future success

- Initial failures often lead to unexpected opportunities

- The same skills that drive success in one area can be applied to others

2. The Power of Redirection

- Passion and discipline are transferable across different pursuits

- Success often comes from redirecting energy rather than starting over

- Adaptability is crucial for long-term achievement

3. Mindset Matters

- Maintaining enthusiasm through failure is crucial

- Self-doubt can be transformed into motivation

- The right mental approach can turn setbacks into comebacks

4. The Role of GRAND SLAM Elements

- Different situations require different combinations of elements

- Success comes from harmonizing available elements

- Not every element needs to be present for success

5. Pattern Recognition

- Understanding personal patterns of success and failure

- Learning to identify transferable skills and strengths

- Recognizing when to persist and when to pivot

These lessons demonstrate that success isn't about avoiding strikeouts but about maintaining the courage and determination to keep stepping up to the plate, being ready for the next opportunity.

5th Inning

From Summer Student to Vice President – A Journey of Consistency, Innovation, and Unexpected Curveballs

---

"Opportunity is missed by most people because it is dressed in overalls and looks like work."
— Thomas Edison

Learning Objectives:

After reading this chapter, you will:

- Understand how seemingly modest beginnings can lead to transformative career opportunities

- Learn how innovative approaches to data management can create competitive advantages

- Recognize the value of mentorship in professional development.

- Understand how technology adoption can revolutionize traditional industries

- Appreciate the role of systematic data collection in business success.

- Identify how adaptability and continuous learning contribute to career advancement

- Comprehend the impact of market dynamics on career opportunities

The Beginning of a Winning Season: Singles and Doubles Galore

While I was experiencing my renaissance in university, I also believed I needed to get office-related job skills. But where to start? My recent resume would have included wannabe rock star and part-time cab driver as experiences. Not very compelling.

At this point, my father was the embodiment of the traditional path of corporate success. For over 25 years, he built his career at A.E. LePage, Canada's largest real estate brokerage firm, which at the time employed more than 8,000 people.

A.E. LePage, founded in 1913 by Albert Edward LePage, was a pioneering Canadian real estate brokerage company that significantly influenced the evolution of the industry. Initially known as "A.E. LePage, Bungalow Specialist," the firm expanded its services and operations over the decades.

The journey of my father, Doug Henderson, was a testament to steady progression and consistent achievement. Starting in residential sales, he established himself as a top producer. Then, in a bold move, he switched to industrial sales, essentially starting over. Through dedication and hard work, he again rose to the top of his field, eventually earning promotion to Vice President and General Manager of the Industrial Division.

While this was a classic success story of climbing the corporate ladder, the real estate profession wasn't highly regarded in those days, unlike today's perception of the industry. My father, perhaps influenced by this view, hoped I would pursue what were then considered more prestigious careers, such as medicine or law. His aspirations for me reflected the values of that era, when traditional professions carried more social status than real estate roles.

After exhausting my job search options for a summer position, I turned to my father for help. Having abandoned my music career aspirations and committed to returning to school, I had begun to rebuild his trust. Though he had reservations about me entering the real estate industry, my desperate situation led him to make an introduction to William Moore, the head of the Office Leasing Division at A.E. LePage. Thanks to my father's respected position within the company, I was offered a summer position. It turns out that your network early in your career includes family.

That first day I stepped into A.E. LePage's offices as a summer student marked the beginning of what would become a transformative journey. While I couldn't have known it then, this opportunity would lay the foundation for my entire business career. What started as a temporary position born of necessity would ultimately shape my professional trajectory in ways I never could have imagined. In retrospect, this moment perfectly illustrated how seemingly modest beginnings can lead to extraordinary outcomes when combined with consistency and determination.

In office leasing, understanding market dynamics and tenant needs is crucial. The brokerage business involves not only negotiating lease agreements but also comprehensively analyzing space requirements, market trends, and location advantages. This sector demands consistent engagement with clients to ensure their evolving needs are met and that they remain competitive within their industries.

I discovered that office leasing operates with a distinct rhythm. Tenants typically sign leases for five to ten years, and as the lease expiration date nears, they begin evaluating their options. In the early days of the industry, prospecting was a hands-on endeavor; salespeople would personally reach out to tenants. The information gathered during this process was often hastily jotted down and stored away, with follow-up systems that were surprisingly rudimentary, akin to keeping score on a scrap of paper.

Enter Gordon Gray, a trained accountant who became LePage's transformative player. Gordon was recruited by the then President Brian McGee to transform the company and set it up for future growth.

Gordon is credited for adding or accelerating many parts of the commercial components of the company. Specific to this story, he introduced a methodology for systematically collecting and using tenant information. The system was based on the Hollerith tabulating methodology , developed by Herman Hollerith in the late 19th century. While it was primarily designed for processing census data, it laid the groundwork for early customer relationship management (CRM) systems.

In the system introduced by Gordon, information was encoded onto punch cards, with holes representing various characteristics or data points. In the case of LePage, it was how many square feet a particular tenant had, when their lease expired, and what geographic area of the city they were interested in. The cards were organized in what looked like a shoebox, and special instruments, resembling knitting needles, were used to detect the holes in the cards. By inserting these instruments into designated sections, users could filter and sort cards based on specific criteria. Any cards that fell out of the box would meet the defined characteristics.

It was like introducing a sophisticated weather satellite forecasting system to a village still relying on a weathervane atop the old church steeple. Using punch cards and needles to extract data, was unbelievably primitive by today's standards but revolutionary for its time. It was the real estate equivalent of inventing the wheel. Sure, we have Teslas now, but someone had to start with a round rock.

As time progressed, the punch cards in shoeboxes were replaced by early service bureau computers. The challenge was that the information was only as good as the input from our salespeople.

Starting at the Bottom

As a summer student, my job was to fill those information gaps. I was tasked to identify all tenants in every office building and estimate their size in square feet and the relevant lease expiry date. It was like being tasked with scouting every player in a league, without the benefit of modern technology. I developed my own system by starting at the top floor of each building and working my way down, noting tenant names and estimating space usage.

Back at the office, I discovered that the company had existing building files with a considerable amount of information, including 8" by 11" floorplans used for marketing. This gave me an idea. Making photocopies of typical floor plans allowed me to sketch out tenant locations more accurately during surveys. It was like creating a playbook for each building, providing the sales team with a strategic advantage.

The next challenge was gathering contact information. Remember, this was pre-internet. I would use phone books and cold calling, piecing together information from receptionists and other gatekeepers like a detective. By asking about move-in dates, I could estimate lease expiries based on typical lease lengths.

My first summer, I personally surveyed 30 million square feet of office space- roughly equivalent to 520 football fields. I collected information on thousands of companies. What I didn't appreciate was that this was novel information to the brokerage firm. It was the equivalent of the leads from the iconic 1992 movie Glengarry, Glen Ross. The sales team came to know what I was doing and would huddle around me when I returned to the office to find information on prospects that were new to the company. This was a game changer for the entire office.

The program's success led to its expansion, and I found myself managing teams of students in subsequent summers. It was like moving from player to coach, all while still in the minor leagues.

What I didn't realize was what a fortified education I was receiving in understanding the vast inventory of office buildings and tenants in the greater Toronto region. By the end of my tenure as summer student and summer student manager, I had personally surveyed more than 60 million sq ft. When you start at the top of the building and walk down each flight of stairs, stopping on each floor to record the tenants, it creates a mental mind map of the building. Decades later, if someone tells me the address of their offices, I can still picture the image of the building, its location, and at least some of the tenants that were in the building. On this level, I had more knowledge than almost any other salesperson. The lesson that I took away from this is that sometimes tasks which appear menial mask hidden gems and career stepping stones.

An Unlikely Move

As graduation from university approached, I faced a crossroads: continue my education or enter the workforce. That's when William B. Moore entered the picture in a big way. Bill was a legend in the commercial real estate industry, a complex character who defied simple comparisons. He possessed both charisma and deal-making prowess. His ability to read people and markets was reminiscent of the bond traders in Michael Lewis' "Liar's Poker," combining street smarts with analytical acumen.

Bill's presence in a room was electric, like a one-man trading floor transported to the world of commercial real estate. He had the uncanny ability to dissect complex market dynamics and explain them with the clarity of a master storyteller. His negotiations were legendary – not for strong-arm tactics, but for creating win-win scenarios that left all parties feeling they'd struck gold.

Unlike the often-cutthroat world portrayed in financial dramas, Bill's success was built on a foundation of ethical practices and genuine relationships. He was as invested in developing his team as he was in closing deals. In a business where information was power, Bill was surprisingly open, seeing knowledge-sharing to elevate the entire industry.

In a move that shocked me, I was offered the opportunity to be Bill's executive assistant. Up until this point, executive assistants were traditionally secretarial roles, and this appointment would have been an unconventional one for a university graduate. However, the role Bill envisioned wasn't confined to managing his calendar or screening calls; it was a chance to be his apprentice and learn the intricacies of high-stakes real estate from a true maestro. I fully embraced this unique opportunity, ready to absorb every lesson this real estate virtuoso had to offer.

Bill's openness was astounding. On my first day in the new role, he shared details of his personal and financial life, even to the extent of sharing his tax return. His salary was 16 times mine, an eye-opening revelation that was both inspirational and a testament to his effusive character.

Despite my father's initial apprehensions about my career in real estate, a broader dynamic was unfolding during the late 1970s and early 1980s. This period witnessed explosive growth in office space, largely driven by demographic shifts and changing labor market trends. The "Baby Boomer" generation, born between 1946 and 1964, began graduating from universities. They entered the workforce with aspirations for office roles in professional sectors like finance, technology, and administration, rather than the blue-collar jobs of previous generations.

This demographic transition resulted in a significant surge in demand for office space. Companies, eager to attract and accommodate this influx of educated workers, expanded their office footprints, creating modern, collaborative environments tailored to appeal to this new workforce. Consequently, demand for office buildings, especially in urban centers, skyrocketed as firms aimed to establish themselves in prime locations to attract talent.

As the demand outstripped supply, the commercial real estate market experienced steep rent escalations. Inflation during this period exacerbated these rent increases, creating a challenging environment for tenants.

In addition, the prevailing political landscape in Quebec significantly influenced decisions regarding the location of corporate headquarters. The rise of the separatist movement and increasing political instability led many businesses, particularly those based in Montreal, to reassess their futures in the province. This uncertainty prompted numerous corporations to relocate some (or all) of their operations to the Greater Toronto Area (GTA).

This migration not only fueled the demand for office space in Toronto but contributed to the influx of young professionals entering the workforce. As these companies sought to attract talent, they intensified the demand for office environments that catered to the needs of a new generation of employees. The combination of modern office space and a favorable business climate positioned Toronto as a premier destination for businesses.

In this thriving environment, commercial real estate agents earned commissions based on a percentage of gross rents. As rents soared, agents' commissions grew correspondingly, allowing them to achieve income levels previously unheard of. This transformation not only elevated the financial landscape for commercial real estate professionals but also positioned them among the elite earners in the business community, showcasing the lucrative potential of the office leasing market during this era of explosive growth.

Why am I telling you this? Because now top office leasing salespeople were making more money than many doctors, lawyers, and other professionals. Sales managers and vice presidents of divisions were paid a percentage of the revenue and profit brought in by their sales teams. Accordingly, their compensation was also growing exponentially. This combination of a dynamic business environment and elevated income potential solidified my ambition for a career in the commercial real estate business.

The Big Play

My role as Bill's Executive Assistant quickly evolved. I became the gatekeeper of information, prioritizing correspondence and drafting responses. I was a fly on the wall at virtually every meeting, including some very boozy lunches. It was my job to come back to the office and process all the information obtained during the meeting and put the necessary actions in place.

The office leasing division at that time had approximately 35 salespeople, with most agents only able to grab a few minutes of Bill's time. As his right-hand person I learned and emulated his passion for people. He also embraced the mantras of work hard/play hard, make lots of money/spend lots of money, and enjoy life along the way. As a young man at the beginning of his career, every day was a new adventure, and it was a genuine pleasure to come to work.

Then came a really big play: LePage decided to invest heavily in computerizing its prospect and market information systems. This was before CRM systems or software-as-a-service existed. No Salesforce, no Hub Spot, no Microsoft Dynamics. The principal option available to enterprises at the time was to develop a proprietary system.

Bill was chosen to be the inspirational architect of this system, with PricewaterhouseCoopers as our tech team. I found myself in the perfect position to be the project manager, working alongside Bill. It was like being called up to the majors and immediately being put in charge of developing a new playbook.

In university, my foray into computer science was about as deep as a puddle in the Sahara. I took exactly one course that involved punch cards, creating a program to do simple math, a far cry from the digital wizardry we were about to embark upon. This meager background was my entire formal education in computing, a fact that would have most modern tech recruiters reaching for their stress balls.

Yet, in the context of our company at that time, this minimal exposure to programming made me the resident tech guru. It was a classic case of "in the land of the blind, the one-eyed man is king," or perhaps more accurately, "in the land of the abacus, the guy with a simple function calculator is a genius."

The system we developed had three major components: an inventory of office buildings, available space within those buildings, and tenant information. We spent countless hours redesigning how every aspect of the system would work. It was a labor of love. My passion for the project was all-consuming; I found myself working six, often seven days a week, driven by an insatiable desire to see this vision come to life. The long hours flew by, fueled by the excitement of creating something truly groundbreaking. I became so engrossed in the project that I started dreaming in binary and seeing the world in data structures.

Bill's decades of experience in the office leasing industry was a critical element in the success of the system. I would sit in our design meetings where Bill would outline not only how the industry works now but his vision of how it could evolve. While he was not technologically gifted, Bill understood what technology could do. He was also prescient in that he anticipated that what a company had today was not necessarily an indicator of what they would want in the future.

So, Bill's idea was to categorize and capture information about a tenant's future requirements. In addition to office space, it also included geographic preferences. This was a quantum leap in thinking about data capture for office tenants. Being on the ground floor of all these conversations allowed me a unique insight. Because I was working with the programmers to bring these business requirements to life I understood how the technology worked at a very detailed level, unheard of for a real estate professional at that time.

The result of our efforts was one of the first IBM System 36 mini-computer installations in Canada, along with one of the company's first personal computers. This wasn't just a technological upgrade; it was a paradigm shift in how real estate business could be conducted.

The impact of our system was immediate and far-reaching. It garnered an incredible amount of attention from various quarters – the media, our clients, our sales team, and certainly our competitors.

In a moment that still feels surreal, I found my picture on the front page of Canada's most prestigious newspaper, the Globe and Mail's Report on Business. For a young professional who had started as a summer student, this level of recognition was both thrilling and humbling. I half-expected to be asked for autographs at real estate conferences – turns out, "database celebrity" isn't quite as glamorous as rock star, but it certainly comes with better job security.

Our computer system and methodological approach to the leasing business became a cornerstone of our pitch to building owners and tenants alike. It was revolutionary compared to what our competitors were doing. We weren't just offering a service; we were providing a sophisticated, data-driven approach to real estate that was years ahead of its time. In an industry where "cutting-edge technology" often meant a new fax machine, we were showing up with a spaceship.

My role expanded dramatically in the wake of this success. I became the operations manager, overseeing all non-sales staff. But my involvement didn't stop there. Thanks to the unique combination of the deep real estate and technological expertise I had gained from the project, combined with the storytelling capabilities I had honed under Bill Moore's mentorship, I became a centerpiece of significant client pitches. I found myself an indispensable partner to the sales team, able to explain complex systems in accessible terms and demonstrate their practical value to clients.

The success of this project taught me invaluable lessons about the power of innovation, the importance of passion in driving success, and the impact that technology can have when applied thoughtfully to traditional industries. It set the stage for my future career, instilling in me a lifelong appreciation for the transformative potential of technology in business. Perhaps most importantly, it taught me that with enough determination and coffee, you can indeed teach an old industry new tricks.

This experience highlighted a pattern that would repeat throughout my career: success through quick learning and consistent application, rather than relying on deep prior experience. It was like being able to adapt to any position on the field, making me a valuable utility player.

Looking back, I'm amazed at what we accomplished in the early '80s without the advanced technology we have today. It sparked my ongoing passion for how technology can transform businesses, a passion that continues to drive me forward.

Skipping a Level

My exposure to sales leadership came through an unconventional path. While most followed the traditional trajectory of first proving themselves in sales before moving into management, my extensive involvement in operations, technology implementation, and client presentations had given me a unique perspective on the business.

Bill Moore's mentorship had provided me with a front-row seat to sales leadership in action. Working as his executive assistant, I had observed how he motivated the sales team, managed complex deals, and built a high-performance culture. This experience, combined with my growing visibility in the organization and understanding of the industry, led me to view the sales manager role as a natural next step. While unconventional, Bill's continued belief in my potential once again opened doors. Despite my lack of direct sales experience, he supported my move into sales leadership, recognizing that my technical knowledge, operational expertise, and understanding of the business could bring a fresh perspective to the role.

The Work Hard, Play Hard Era: When Martini Lunches met Morning Meetings

The 1980s business culture was shaped by a distinct social dynamic that would be unrecognizable in today's corporate world. I was immersed in this environment early, growing up in what could have been a scene from "Mad Men." My parents' generation considered cocktail hour sacred, and weekend parties were ritualistic social events. The clink of ice in whiskey glasses and the haze of cigarette smoke were as much a part of my childhood landscape as summer vacations and Sunday dinners.

This social framework carried seamlessly into the business world of the 1980s, where the three-martini lunch wasn't just accepted – it was expected. Deals were sealed over drinks, relationships were built at bars, and the line between professional and social life was consistently blurred. The unwritten rule was simple: party as hard as you want, stay out as late as you dare, but your presence at the morning meeting was non-negotiable. I recall a perverse competition among junior executives to see who could arrive earliest after an all-night celebration: a badge of honor that would horrify today's HR departments.

Looking back through the lens of James Clear's Atomic Habits, this behavior perfectly illustrates how habits are shaped by our environment, particularly what he calls "the close, the many, and the powerful." Our habits are influenced by those closest to us (family and close friends), the many (colleagues and industry-wide culture), and the powerful (mentors and senior executives who modeled and rewarded this behavior). The social cues, peer pressure, and cultural norms of the era created an environment where this lifestyle wasn't just tolerated – it was celebrated.

So, it was perhaps predictable that I would mirror this behavior. But the path from social drinking to problematic behavior is often subtle and seductive. Given my early exposure to this lifestyle and my apparent ability to function well despite heavy drinking – regularly winning those unofficial competitions to be first in the office after a night out – I developed a dangerous confidence in my ability to "handle" this lifestyle. My successful management of these situations only reinforced this belief. I could close deals, lead meetings, and drive business growth while maintaining what I saw as a legendary capacity for alcohol.

This self-deception was particularly insidious because it was wrapped in the cultural norms of the time and validated by my professional success. What I didn't recognize then was that these behaviors were creating subtle but significant speed bumps in my career trajectory. Like a high-performance car with slightly misaligned wheels, I was still moving forward rapidly, but the true cost of this misalignment would only become apparent over time. The belief that I could successfully navigate both worlds – high-functioning executive by day, party animal by night – had become deeply embedded in my identity.

To further quote from Atomic Habits, beliefs shape our habits and habits shape our identity. The more I succeeded while maintaining this lifestyle, the more I believed it was sustainable. Breaking free from this cycle would require more than just behavior modification; it would demand a fundamental shift in how I viewed myself. This journey of self-discovery and transformation would become a crucial chapter in my personal and professional development, which we'll explore more deeply in later chapters.

Rewriting My Playbook in the Queen's English: A Mentor's Eloquent Game-Changer

In the grand arena of life, I've been blessed with a dream team of mentors and inspirations. But if there's a LeBron James in this lineup – a true game-changer who transcends the sport and redefines what's possible – it's undoubtedly John O'Bryan.

John was already a seasoned player at LePage when I joined. Born, raised, and educated in the UK, John was a consummate Englishman, with an accent that made whatever he said sound smart, which he invariably was.

Our paths didn't initially intersect on the corporate court; he was off in his native UK, attempting to expand LePage's services across the pond, much like an all-star player on loan to an international team. Meanwhile, I was still in the rookie stages, learning to differentiate between a net and gross lease.

Upon his return to the Canadian major leagues, John joined the Investment Sales Division as a salesperson and ascended the ranks to quickly become one of the company's top salespeople. He landed in a sales leadership position that mirrored my own, though his jersey had far more experience patches sewn onto it.

On the surface, John and I were as different as Earl Grey tea and espresso - one refined and steeped in tradition, the other bold and intense. But beneath these superficial differences, we were both fueled by the same caffeine: a burning passion for excellence and a shared vision of how to win in this high-stakes game of commercial real estate.

John was the visionary, a natural-born slugger in the business world. He strategized big plays and crafted high-level strategies that could change the game in a single swing. His eloquent pitches charmed clients, leaving them eager to sign on the dotted line. John's eyes were always on the distant fences, envisioning home runs where others saw only base hits.

I, on the other hand, was the architect of processes and procedures, the steady infielder ensuring every routine play was executed flawlessly. I drafted organizational blueprints with the meticulous detail of a groundskeeper preparing the diamond, ensuring every base was covered and every line was clearly drawn. My focus was on the fundamentals, the day-to-day operations that kept our business running like a well-oiled machine.

When executive positions opened, it was as clear as daylight to me that John should take the head coach role. But in a move that defies typical corporate hierarchies and protocol, he insisted we be equal co-captains, with identical contracts and compensation. This was absolutely stunning to me. He was a few years my senior and I regarded his capabilities with the reverence rightfully reserved for superstars. I would have been content playing the reliable second to his all-star lead in our commercial real estate team.

At first, I insisted, if not persisted, in explaining all the reasons he should receive a more senior role and compensation. I do admit that I started to question my own sanity about trying to convince someone to pay me less. John persistently explained that his vision of a perfect relationship would be one of equals. He did not want there to be any reason to compare effort and compensation going forward. With the jubilance of someone who has just won the lottery, I accepted his gracious offer.

John's wisdom in this decision was like a well-executed game strategy: its true value only became apparent as the game progressed. Thanks to his approach, I contributed to our partnership with the enthusiasm of a rookie getting his chance in the big leagues.

We recognized our complementary skills like two halves of a perfectly balanced ledger. John's ability to see the forest was perfectly balanced by my obsession for naming each tree, categorizing its leaves, and optimizing its photosynthesis process.

As we navigated the world of commercial real estate together, John's mentorship became my secret weapon, like having a direct line to the coach's playbook. His guidance wasn't just about closing deals; it was about understanding the game at a deeper level, reading the field, and anticipating the moves of our competitors three steps ahead. Our partnership proved that in the corporate world, having both the dreamer and the doer, the disruptor and the developer can create a whole that is greater than the sum of the parts.

John's passion to demonstrate leadership was palpable. He thrived in the arena of public speaking, turning presentations into performances that would make TED Talk organizers weep with joy.

His negotiation skills were so sharp, I half expected to see him leaving meetings with the other party's watch, wallet, and a signed confession.

Meanwhile, my idea of a grand slam was crafting foolproof quality assurance systems that caught every error before it could cross the plate.

But here's where the magic happened: we didn't just stick to our lanes like obedient rule followers. Oh no, we were more like those brave little robot vacuums, venturing curiously into each other's territories. I'd watch John work his wizardry with the awe of a rookie witnessing a perfect game. His way with words was like watching a verbal cricket match: elegant, strategic, and utterly baffling to the uninitiated.

John, in turn, would appreciate my meticulously designed procedures and how I could transform a chaotic brainstorm into an actionable strategy faster than a double play.

This mutual admiration wasn't just about spectating from the sidelines. It was our spring training for personal growth. By observing John's oratory skills, I gradually improved from a nervous speech reader to someone speaking almost at his level.

This partnership taught us that in the business world, it's not about knowing when to tag in your pinch runner. When a task played to our strengths, we'd step up to the plate like a cleanup hitter with bases loaded. But we also knew that sometimes, the best way to improve is to face a pitcher you've never seen before.

John's counsel wasn't always what I wanted to hear. There were times when his suggestions seemed as baffling as cricket rules to an American audience. "Trust the process," he'd say, sounding more like a Zen master than a business mentor. But lo and behold, following his advice was unconventional, perhaps, but undeniably effective.

But it wasn't all serious business and strategic maneuvers. John had a knack for lighting the mood with his distinctly British humor, dropping witticisms drier than a martini at cocktail hour. His well-timed quips were like those rare, refreshing rain delays in a tense game – a chance to reset, refocus, and remember why we loved playing in the first place.

Looking back, I realize John's coaching style was less about giving me a playbook and more about teaching me to read the field. He was developing my business acumen, honing my ability to read situations, adapt to changing conditions, and make split-second decisions under pressure.

Without his guidance, I might have been stuck in the minor leagues of my profession, forever chasing the elusive call-up to the big show. Instead, thanks to John's mentorship, I found myself not just playing in the majors but gunning for the MVP title in my field.

Coach Robbins: Transforming the Game

In the early innings of my business career, a late-night infomercial caught my eye like as bright as the lights in a stadium. It was Anthony (Tony) Robbins, pitching his 30-day Personal Power audio tape series. For those born in the digital age, audio tapes were the vinyl records of the spoken word world, predecessors to CDs and streaming, relics of a time when inspiration came in plastic cassettes.

Something about Robbins' message resonated with me, like a perfectly pitched idea. I thought it would be a game-changer for both my wife and me, so I stepped up to the plate and ordered the tapes. Over the next few weeks, my daily commute transformed into a mobile classroom, with Robbins as my unseen coach.

The content was a comprehensive playbook for life: goal setting, overcoming limiting beliefs, developing a positive mindset, improving relationships, achieving financial success, and enhancing physical health. To say it was transformative would be like calling a no-hitter "a pretty good game." It sparked a fire in me that I couldn't help but spread to my colleagues. Soon, I and members of the sales team were signing up in small groups for Tony Robbins live events, like rookies eager for spring training.

As our enthusiasm grew, I began to see the potential for this programming to revolutionize our sales team. It was then that I discovered Tony's "Power to Influence" VHS-based video training programs (and no, we won't dig into the Betamax vs. VHS debate here).

Released in the early '90s, this training program was the major league of personal development, sold through authorized value-added consulting companies. The series, consisting of multiple video sessions, was like a masterclass in personal influence and communication skills, the very tools critical for sales success. Our sessions were facilitated by Dale Becks, an authorized Tony Robbins trainer who augmented the video content with exercises, roleplaying, and homework, much like a coach runs drills between games.

We started with a test run of 12 salespeople, and the results were so impressive that we expanded the training to all 200 salespeople in the Greater Toronto region. The outcome was nothing short of miraculous. A common language emerged among the group, centered around core elements like limiting and empowering beliefs. It enhanced the performance of everyone, from the greenest rookie to the most seasoned veteran.

Sure, some people were put off by Tony's larger-than-life personality. It was like watching a motivational Babe Ruth call his shot. But even the skeptics couldn't argue with the results. Everyone managed to take the lessons from the program and incorporate them into their personal style, like players adapting a new technique to their swing.

The financial results, both for individuals and the company as a whole, became self-evident. People were winning more mandates, closing more deals, and generally achieving more success. It was as if the whole team had suddenly found their sweet spot.

Years later, when I catch up with alumni from those days, they all remember this training with the fond reverence usually reserved for a championship season. Many consider it some of the most important fundamental training they ever received in sales or have ever received since.

Power Talk: Swing from Vine to Vine

One of Tony's other programs, Power Talk, featured interviews with interesting people, like scouting reports for success. One guest was Paul Pilzer, author of Unlimited Wealth: The Theory and Practice of Economic Alchemy. Pilzer's interview was so compelling that I immediately bought his book, eager to dive deeper into his ideas.

Pilzer's concept of "Unlimited Wealth" in the context of '90s commercial real estate was like discovering a new way to play the game. It suggested that technological advancements could significantly enhance the value and utilization of real estate assets. As technology evolved, it enabled more efficient use of office spaces, facilitated the rise of new industries, and allowed for the global expansion of businesses. The potential for wealth creation in commercial real estate was no longer limited by traditional factors but was increasingly driven by how well properties could adapt to a rapidly evolving, technology-driven economy.

Inspired by this new perspective, I reached out to Paul to invite him as a guest speaker at a real estate industry event in Toronto. It was a bold move, like swinging for the fences with two strikes, but it paid off. Not only did Paul agree, but his presentation was a home run. This led to a business friendship and further speaking engagements, including an intimate company event for our top performers.

During one of these events, I shared with Paul how impactful Tony Robbins' program had been for our sales team. Little did I know, this conversation would set up the ultimate power play.

Paul, being close to Tony and a regular speaker at his events, offered to speak to Tony on my behalf. It was like having an all-star vouch for you to the league MVP. Leveraging this connection and appealing to Tony's charitable side, we managed to secure him as a speaker for a comparatively small group event: the Society of Industrial and Office Realtors annual event in Hawaii.

The event organizers were stunned. It was a major boost to my profile in the organization, and I was thrilled at the positive impact Tony would have on my colleagues from around the world.

Meeting Your Heroes: An Unexpected Masterclass in Authenticity

Then came a moment that felt like destiny had thrown me a perfect pitch - I was offered the chance to ride in the limousine picking up Tony from the airport. This wasn't just any car ride; it was an hour and a half of one-on-one time with someone who had profoundly influenced my approach to business and life.

They say you should never meet your heroes, that the reality rarely lives up to the legend. But my experience with Tony Robbins proved to be a remarkable exception. Having immersed myself in his teachings for years (consuming every book, audio program, and video training available), I had internalized his principles so thoroughly that I found myself in an unusual position: I had very few questions for the man himself. His teachings had become such an integral part of my professional toolkit that I felt I knew exactly what he would say in almost any situation.

What struck me most during this intimate conversation wasn't his larger-than-life personality or his famous energy; it was his singular focus on serving his audience. Instead of engaging in small talk or sharing war stories, Tony spent the entire ride asking detailed questions about the upcoming event and audience. "What are their biggest challenges? What outcomes would make this event transformational for them? How can I customize my message to create maximum impact?" His genuine concern for delivering value was palpable. Here was someone who had spoken to millions, yet he approached this relatively small gathering of real estate professionals with the same intensity and commitment as a stadium event.

This experience revealed the true character behind the public persona. It wasn't just that Tony practiced what he preached – it was that his teachings were simply an extension of who he was at his core. The man who had built an empire helping others reach their potential was, even in private moments, completely focused on how he could serve others. It was a powerful lesson in authentic leadership and a reminder that, sometimes, meeting your heroes can enhance your admiration for them, especially when they prove to be even more genuine than their public image suggests.

The pinnacle of this journey was introducing Tony to a room full of the top 400 realtors in North America. His presentation was, predictably, phenomenal, like watching a veteran pitcher throw a perfect game.

Looking back, this series of events,from that late-night infomercial to the limo ride with Tony, were a string of singles, doubles, and triples that added up to a winning season. It's a testament to the power of continuous learning, networking, and seizing opportunities – the very principles Tony Robbins champions.

Pitching Beyond the Bullpen: Boardroom Broadway

Our journey into the realm of influence had begun with the "Power to Influence" program, which had armed us with formidable skills for one-on-one interactions. We were like expert pitchers, able to throw a perfect strike in a bullpen session. But the real game was played on a much larger field, and we needed to expand our playbook.

Commercial real estate, with its high stakes and hefty price tags, often demanded performances worthy of the World Series. Our deals weren't just being closed in cozy offices; they were being pitched in boardrooms, where executives and decision-makers sat like a panel of stern umpires, ready to call any misstep. It was clear that our team needed to step up to the plate and deliver grand slam presentations that would leave even the toughest critics cheering.

I saw this skills gap as a crucial weakness in our lineup. It was like having a team of excellent batters who froze up when the stadium lights came on. We needed to transform our players into all-stars who could perform under pressure, turning every pitch into an opportunity to knock it out of the park. We did not need to look any further than John O'Bryan for our model of what great presenting looked like. But how do you lead that transformation?

Enter (or in this case re-enter) Dale Becks, our trainer extraordinaire. I approached her with the idea to create a presentation training course for our salespeople, based on the Power to Influence training we had already received.

Our new training program was like spring training on steroids (the legal kind, of course). We focused on making our messages not just clear, but compelling, turning every presentation into a highlight reel of persuasive plays. But the real game-changer? We tackled the curveballs head-on.

You know those questions that make you wish for a sudden power outage or an impromptu fire drill? The ones about why your company is better than the competition or why our fees make eyebrows disappear into hairlines? We didn't just prepare for them; we turned them into our secret weapons.

We crowdsourced the most dreaded questions. It was like creating a "Greatest Hits" album of corporate nightmares. Then, in a move that would make any improv coach proud, we brainstormed, refined, and polished our responses until they shone brighter than a newly waxed office floor.

Our training sessions transformed into a kind of corporate theatre. We role-played scenarios that would make Broadway actors break character. People practiced fielding those tough questions like infielders drilling double plays. Soon, what was once dreaded became anticipated. It was as if the mere sight of a raised hand sent our team into a state of excited readiness, like a batter who's just been thrown their favorite pitch.

But wait, there's more! (As they say in those late-night infomercials). We didn't stop at just nailing the Q&A. Oh no, we went full Broadway.

I've always believed that a dash of drama can turn a good presentation into a showstopper. If you can educate while entertaining, you've hit the persuasion jackpot.

So, we started dreaming up approaches that added visuals that popped, transitions that wowed, and storytelling that rivaled the best TED talks. Our presentations became multimedia experiences that engaged not just the mind, but all the senses (including taste and smell).

Wait a minute, we were real estate salespeople, not Madison Avenue Mad Men. Our idea of creativity usually peaked at choosing between eggshell and ivory for our business cards. But sometimes, the universe throws you a curveball so perfect, you'd be a fool not to swing at it.

Enter Declan Sinclair, a young man so bursting with creativity and enthusiasm, he made a firecracker look like a candle. This whippersnapper wanted a job in marketing. Marketing? In our firm? That was like asking for a job as a rodeo clown in an accounting office. We didn't have a marketing department, and our budget for "creative endeavors" was roughly the cost of a pack of sticky notes.

But then, like a bolt of lightning striking a golf club, an idea hit me. Why not set this creative dynamo loose as an independent contractor, with us as his guinea pig – I mean, his inaugural client? It was like giving Picasso his first set of crayons and saying, "Go nuts, kid. Just try to color inside the lines of our corporate logo."

Declan, bless his adventurous soul, took to this idea like a duck to water. Or more accurately, like a caffeinated squirrel to an obstacle course. Before we knew it, our staid, boring collateral materials were transformed. Brochures that once put people to sleep faster than a zoning law seminar suddenly popped with color and verve. Our presentations started looking less like sedated PowerPoints and more like Vegas opening acts.

One example stands out. Picture this: a client is preparing to interview the top real estate firms. It's like "The Bachelor," but instead of roses, they're handing out million-dollar contracts. The burning question on every client's mind: "What makes your firm different?" It's the corporate equivalent of asking, "So, tell me about yourself," on a first date.

That's when Declan, our resident mad genius, cooked up an idea so audacious, it made Don Draper look like a timid schoolboy. He created a custom box, emblazoned with the client's logo, filled with... wait for it... muffins. But not just any muffins. Oh no, this was a muffin-based metaphor so on-the-nose, it risked causing blunt force trauma.

Inside this box of baked goods was a collection of bland, identical muffins, the kind you'd expect to find at a corporate meeting where fun goes to die.

But in the center, like a king among peasants, sat one muffin. This wasn't just any muffin. This was the Beyoncé of muffins: larger, more attractive, and ready to steal the show. Each muffin bore a tiny flag with the logo from each of our competitors. And guess whose logo was strutting its stuff on the star muffin? Ours, baby!

Now, this wasn't just some half-baked stunt (pun absolutely intended). Oh no, this was part of a presentation so carefully orchestrated, it would make Mozart weep with envy. We'd stride into that boardroom, confidence oozing from our pores, and declare we were about to show why our firm was the cream of the crop. Then, with the dramatic flair of a magician revealing his final trick, we'd present The Box.

Imagine the clients' faces as they opened a box bearing their own logo, only to find this pastry-based corporate drama playing out before their eyes. It was confusion, amusement, and "aha!" all rolled into one glorious moment of realization. This visual gag set the stage perfectly for us to then lay out, in mouth-watering detail, exactly why we were the big muffin on campus. Make no mistake, our presentation had the rich content that our clients wanted; we just delivered it in a more interesting fashion.

There's an old showbiz saying: "Love me or hate me, just remember me." Well, let me tell you, we were about as forgettable as a fire alarm at a world series game. While our competitors were still stuck in the land of monotonous monologues and sleep-inducing slides, we were putting on a show that rivaled Broadway (okay, maybe off-Broadway, but still).

But perhaps the most beautiful part of all this? The confidence these presentations instilled in our team. They went from approaching presentations with the trepidation of a rookie facing a seasoned pitcher to volunteering for them like they were stepping up to bat in the bottom of the ninth. They strode into boardrooms not just prepared, but excited. They saw tough questions not as threats, but as opportunities to shine. Our team transformed from a group of individuals into a cohesive, high-performing unit that could adapt to any situation, any audience, any challenge.

Clients went from checking their watches to asking for encores. We turned what could have been dry, data-heavy pitches into memorable experiences that left lasting impressions. It was as if we'd taken the often-monotonous game of commercial real estate and added a few crowd-pleasing curveballs for variety.

Our enthusiasm was contagious. The team's newfound confidence and our creative approach not only impressed clients but also fostered a sense of trust and connection. We managed to make complex real estate discussions not just informative, but genuinely engaging. At the end of the day, people prefer to deal with those they know, like and trust. This approach was a way to accelerate that experience, turning what could have been a long, drawn-out season into a fast-paced form of speed dating.

The Art of Handling Provocative Dialogue

One of the most valuable lessons I learned about handling conflict came from an unexpected source: a media training session at a Society of Industrial and Office Realtors conference. The facilitator, a former media trainer who had worked with high-profile figures including President Ronald Reagan, demonstrated a powerful approach to handling confrontational conversations. It would prove invaluable throughout my career.

The Power of Provocation

The session began with a dramatic demonstration. The facilitator, interviewing a female professional from the audience, launched into a deliberately provocative question: "As a member of the Society of Industrial and Office Realtors, you are among the elite and privileged people in the world, here at this lavish resort on an all-expense-paid junket. How does it feel to be the Imelda Marcos of real estate?"

The volunteer's response illustrated common reactive patterns:

- Defensive denial of the accusations

- Repetition of inflammatory language

- Engagement with the provocative premise

- Loss of professional composure

The Reframing Revolution

The facilitator then introduced a revolutionary concept: instead of responding to the actual question, ask yourself, "If this person was a wonderful person and had my highest intentions in mind, what question would they be asking me?" This simple but powerful reframe transforms hostile questions into constructive dialogue opportunities. The facilitator also suggested that in responding, you first pause and take time to collect your thoughts. Then smile in a way that expresses that you are in a calm and pleasant state and finally answer the rewarded question from above.

As a group, we went on considering this common confrontation in commercial real estate:

Original Question: "You commercial real estate salespeople are all the same. Your fees are ridiculous and outrageously high. How can you guys get away with this kind of highway robbery?"

Reframed Question: "In making my decision about selecting a commercial real estate professional, I would like to know what makes you unique among your peers and how your fee relates to the services provided."

The reframing of the question can generally be solely in your own mind. Your answer will be different than the initially posed question. In some cases, you can restate the initial question back to the person who asked it to build rapport and gain alignment. One version might be, "I appreciate that in trying to decide, you are really trying to best understand the differences between the various firms competing for your business. Let me explain why I believe our company is uniquely suited to handle your situation, and how our fees are a fraction of the value we provide."

The Power of Positive Assumption

This approach offers several advantages:

1. De-escalating the Exchange: By pausing and smiling, it brings about a sense of calm.

2. Emotional Distance: By assuming positive intent, you maintain professional composure.

3. Constructive Direction: Reframing guides the conversation toward productive dialogue.

4. Professional Control: You maintain leadership of the discussion.

5. Value Focus: The conversation shifts from price to value.

6. Relationship Building: Tension decreases as dialogue improves.

Practical Application

The technique requires practice but can be applied in various situations:

1. Fee Negotiations

   Original: "Your commission is outrageous!"

   Reframe: "You're interested in understanding the value you'll receive for your investment?"

2. Market Challenges

Original: "I am not getting the results I want. You're not doing enough!"

Reframe: "You'd like to understand our strategy for achieving your goals in this market?"

3. Timeline Pressure

Original: "Why is this taking so long? Are you even working on this?"

Reframe: "You'd like an update on our progress and timeline?"

The Business Impact

This approach transforms potentially confrontational situations into opportunities for:

- Deeper client relationships

- Better understanding of client needs

- More productive negotiations

- Professional reputation enhancement

- Long-term business development

Mastering the Technique

Success with this approach requires:

- Practice in low-stakes situations
- Role play with colleagues
- Preparation for common challenges
- Emotional self-awareness
- Quick thinking and adaptation
- Genuine commitment to understanding

Legacy Learning

This lesson has served me well beyond media training or real estate negotiations. It's a fundamental skill for:

- Leadership communication
- Conflict resolution
- Team management
- Client relationships
- Strategic negotiations

The ultimate power of this approach lies not just in handling difficult conversations better, but in transforming potentially adversarial relationships into collaborative partnerships. By assuming positive intent and reframing provocative questions, we create opportunities for meaningful dialogue and mutual understanding.

Team Synergy: Redefining Success in a Commission-Driven World

While working on the transformation with the sales teams, John and I identified a key weakness in the traditional commercial real estate brokerage model. The commission-based structure of the industry encouraged individual hustle, but it also created a "lone wolf" mentality that sometimes worked against the firm's and clients' best interests. Individual brokers, protective of their commissions, would often tackle complex deals alone, even when they lacked certain crucial skills or experience. This approach led to inconsistent results and missed opportunities. It was like sending a pitcher to bat in a crucial game situation when you had power hitters available on the bench.

We adopted a non-traditional (at the time) approach: proactive team formation based on deal assessment. Rather than waiting for brokers to fail or struggle, we would evaluate each opportunity upfront and strategically assemble teams that combined complementary skills and experience levels. For instance, if a junior broker had strong analytical skills but lacked presentation experience, we'd pair them with a senior broker known for their pitch abilities.

Initially, this met resistance; brokers were understandably protective of their leads and commissions. However, through careful persuasion and early successes, we demonstrated that a smaller piece of a deal won was far better than 100% of a lost opportunity. Senior brokers, in particular, embraced this system, seeing both the chance to mentor junior colleagues and participate in more deals. The result was transformative: our win rate increased significantly, and we created a collaborative culture that became a competitive advantage in the marketplace. This approach exemplified the Consistency Effect by creating reliable, repeatable success through systematic teamwork rather than relying on individual heroics.

Over the following year, our team knocked it out of the park, winning far more than our fair share of assignments. Each victory boosted the confidence of both the individual players and the entire squad, emboldening us to stretch our ambitions even further. We were building a championship caliber team.

As we continued to rack up wins, the synergy within our team became palpable. We were no longer just a collection of individual players; we had become a well-oiled machine, each person knowing their role and executing it with precision. The impact of these successes rippled far beyond the confines of our office. Clients began to see us not just as service providers, but as trusted advisors – and our reputation grew, in the major leagues of high-stakes deals.

As I watched our team evolve, I couldn't help but feel a sense of pride. The self-confidence in our people had risen like a baseball soaring out of a stadium. We had taken the "Power to Influence" and amplified it, creating a symphony of persuasion where once there was a solo performance. We had turned our sales team into a group of corporate rock stars, capable of wowing any audience, handling any heckler, and leaving every venue (or boardroom) wanting more. And in doing so, we discovered that the real power of influence doesn't just lie in what you say, but in how you say it, how you show it, and how you make your audience feel it. You need to be the big muffin in a box of small ones to really rise to the top.

GRAND SLAM Elements

As is our practice, we will look at this through the most relevant GRAND SLAM elements to talk about what worked and what could have been done better.

Great Idea:

- Transforming traditional sales presentations into engaging experiences.

- The innovative muffin box concept as an example of differentiation.

- Creating proactive team formation based on skill assessment and chemistry.

- Combining presentation training with creative marketing.

Resilience:

- Overcoming initial resistance to team-based approaches.

- Transforming fear of tough questions into opportunities to differentiate our service.

- Helping team members overcome presentation anxiety.

Action:

- Implementing comprehensive presentation training

- Bringing in Dale Becks and Declan Sinclair as catalysts for change.

- Taking decisive steps to address the skills gap.

- Proactively forming teams based on opportunity assessment.

Network:

- Building collaborative teams instead of fostering lone-wolf mentality.

- Creating synergistic relationships between senior and junior brokers.

- Developing strong client connections through engaging presentations.

Discipline:

- Consistent practice and preparation for presentations.

- Regular training sessions and role-playing.

- Systematic approach to team formation and deal assessment.

Skill:

- Developing presentation and public speaking abilities.

- Enhancing creative marketing capabilities.

- Building expertise in team collaboration.

- Improving question handling and audience engagement.

Mentors:

- John O'Bryan serving as a presentation role model.

- Senior brokers mentoring junior colleagues.

- Dale Becks' ongoing training and development role.

The Power of Purpose: Building Networks Through Giving

"The best networking doesn't feel like networking at all." This truth became evident throughout my career as I discovered that the most valuable professional relationships often grew from genuine community involvement rather than explicit networking events.

The Junior Achievement Journey

My first introduction to strategic volunteering came through William Dimma, LePage's president. Bill was on the Board of Governors of Junior Achievement as well as many other prominent organizations. Junior Achievement's mandate was to empower young people to succeed in a global economy by providing real-world learning experiences that focus on financial literacy, entrepreneurship, and work readiness. Through hands-on programs and engagement with business professionals, JA equips students with the knowledge, skills, and mindset needed to make smart academic and economic choices while preparing them for future career success.

One of Bill's jobs as Governor was to find emerging leaders in his company who could become members of the Board of Directors. When Bill invited me to join the Board of JA, I was flattered. While the Board of Directors consisted primarily of vice presidents from various organizations, the Board of Governors read like a who's who of Canadian business leadership, featuring CEOs from the nation's largest companies.

Influence Without Authority

What I came to realize is that JA was a working board. Specifically, members of the board of directors would take active roles in the development and implementation of programs. In fact, we were part-time senior staff members dedicated to the cause. Large committees were established to capitalize on the talent from the Board of Directors. I was quickly recruited to co-chair one of the initiatives called the "Economics of Staying in School" (ESIS). This program was designed to help students understand the long-term financial benefits of completing their education. It focuses on how staying in school can lead to higher earnings, greater career opportunities, and improved quality of life. The program typically includes lessons on the importance of education for economic success, budgeting, and career planning. By offering real-world insights into personal finance and the economic impact of education, the program aims to inspire students to value their education and make informed decisions about their future.

The program was targeted to students in grade 8 because at the age of 14 they could elect to leave high school with their parents' permission. The idea was to encourage them to stay in school as an investment in their future employability.

The group had a lofty goal to create an ESIS program in every school in the greater Toronto region, roughly 1100 schools. It seemed like a daunting task, and it was my first real experience with setting a "big hairy audacious goal" (BHAG). What I came to learn from this experience was that BHAGs have a unique way of becoming the NorthStar for group direction and the compelling "why" the group needs to get there. It was also a phenomenal experience with something that many people call "influence without authority." Here I was, co-chairing a committee with people that were at my level or higher in their respective organizations. There was a lot of work to do, and my job was to persuade them to do it. It was an incredible experience in managing people and a talent that has served me extensively throughout my entire career.

When you lead with genuine passion for a cause, meaningful connections naturally follow. My experience with JA also taught me a valuable lesson about relationship building: authentic networking flourishes when your primary focus is creating positive impact.

By approaching volunteer work with sincere dedication to the mission, I found that professional relationships evolved organically. The conversations shifted naturally from our shared commitment to financial education to exploring potential business collaborations – but only after establishing that foundation of trust through meaningful service.

This organic approach has proven far more effective than traditional networking tactics. When your priority is contributing value through volunteerism, business relationships develop authentically as a natural extension of shared values and mutual respect.

From Industry Involvement to Leadership

As my career progressed, I became involved with the Society of Industrial and Office Realtors (SIOR), eventually rising to become Chairman of Canada. Similarly, serving on the board of the Industrial Development Research Council (IDC, later Cornet) provided opportunities to contribute while building relationships with industry leaders.

Connecting with the Business Community

My early success leading Junior Achievement initiatives, combined with growing responsibilities at LePage, built my confidence in leading complex projects. However, it was my involvement with the Toronto Board of Trade that truly transformed my leadership capabilities and understanding of large-scale influence.

The first major challenge came when I was asked to chair a committee tasked with uniting 29 competing municipalities and the private sector into what would become the Greater Toronto Marketing Alliance (GTMA). Each municipality had its own economic development office, budget, and priorities. Convincing these autonomous entities to work together required a delicate balance of diplomacy and persistence. This project became a master class in "influence without authority," the art of achieving alignment without direct control.

The success of the GTMA led to an even more ambitious assignment: chairing the committee focused on Toronto's waterfront development. This initiative brought together three levels of government (municipal, provincial, and federal) along with numerous private sector stakeholders. The goal of the BOT Waterfront Taskforce was to ensure private sector input into the establishment of the corporation that would ultimately transform hundreds of acres of underutilized waterfront land into a catalyst for regional growth.

These achievements led to my appointment to the Board of Trade's executive committee, where I had the opportunity to shape policy and drive initiatives at an even higher level. Each role built upon the previous one, creating a compound effect of increasing influence and impact and adding multiple new connections to my network.

This period perfectly illustrated the Consistency Effect in action. Success didn't come from grand gestures or dramatic pronouncements. Instead, it emerged from countless meetings, careful relationship building, and persistent effort to align diverse interests toward common goals. It was also an opportunity for all my new connections to see my leadership in action. The network of relationships and depth of experience gained through this volunteer work proved invaluable throughout my career, creating opportunities and insights that continued to pay dividends decades later.

Seizing Opportunity: The Birth of a Real Estate Institution

Sometimes the best opportunities appear when others see only challenges. This proved true in 1992 when entrepreneur George Przybylowski approached industry leaders with his vision for a new real estate event. At the time, The Property Forum was a major annual conference attended by senior real estate executives from across Canada since its inception in 1971. Produced by McLean Hunter, the conference dominated the real estate market landscape, and most industry veterans dismissed the viability of anyone launching a competitor to this event. While my colleagues saw redundancy, I recognized an opportunity to help build something significant from the ground up.

This early decision to support The Real Estate Forum as a fledgling venture proved transformative. By securing LePage as its inaugural sponsor and recruiting William Dimma as the first chairperson, we provided the crucial credibility needed for a new event to gain traction. This early support demonstrated a fundamental principle in business: being present at the creation of something meaningful often yields dividends far beyond initial expectations.

What began as a modest, 300-person, one-day gathering quickly evolved into Canada's premier real estate industry event. In the early days, I carved out the role of chair of the organizing committee. I recruited various industry leaders including landlords, tenants, investors, lenders, and brokers. The role of the organizing committee was to assist George and his team in generating the appropriate and timely topics for panel discussions and the suggested subject matter experts to speak on these topics.

The Forum created a comprehensive platform that brought together stakeholders from across the industry to address challenges and share insights. The programming featured influential keynote speakers addressing pressing industry issues, while specialized sessions and panels catered to specific interests and issues. The success of the Forum in Toronto drove its expansion to other gateway cities including Vancouver, Calgary, Edmonton, Montreal, and Ottawa, with each regional event maintaining a national perspective while addressing local market dynamics. I was able to have my colleagues from LePage in each of the markets to assume similar roles to mine and assist George and his team in producing a relevant program, recruit appropriate speakers, and assist in marketing the event to the right target groups.

My involvement with the Forum transformed my role in the industry in unexpected ways. Instead of pursuing hard-to-reach executives, they began seeking me out. I became a gateway to speaking opportunities and developed a reputation as an industry connector, building trust through consistent value delivery. This experience taught me invaluable lessons about network building through authentic engagement and sustained commitment.

The Real Estate Forum's evolution from modest beginnings to the industry's flagship event and cornerstone was truly remarkable and I was proud to have been a part of it. The relationships formed through this venture have lasted a lifetime, not because networking was the goal, but because shared purpose created authentic connections that stand the test of time.

The Power of Purpose: A Lifetime of Network Building Through Service

Looking back over decades of volunteer work – from Junior Achievement to The Real Estate Forum – one truth stands crystal clear: the most valuable professional relationships grow from seeds planted in genuine service. Throughout my career, I've discovered that authentic contribution to meaningful causes creates connections far stronger than any traditional networking approach could achieve. When you lead with sincere commitment to a common purpose, business relationships develop naturally as a byproduct of shared values and mutual respect. Whether helping launch what would become Canada's premier real estate forum or serving on nonprofit boards, the pattern remains consistent: focus first on making a real difference, and the network will build itself.

This approach requires patience – it's more marathon than sprint – but it creates relationships built on trust rather than transactions. The professionals I've met through volunteer work have become not just business contacts but trusted colleagues and often friends, precisely because our connections were forged in the pursuit of something larger than individual gain. When you focus on giving rather than getting, you create relationships that stand the test of time and often yield opportunities you never could have anticipated when you first raised your hand to help.

Bottom of the 5th Inning:

This chapter traces a transformative journey from summer student to industry innovator at A.E. LePage, demonstrating how modest beginnings and consistent effort can lead to remarkable achievements. What started as basic data collection of Toronto office buildings evolved into pioneering one of Canada's first computerized CRM systems, revolutionizing how the industry managed market intelligence and client relationships.

Under the mentorship of William Moore and later John O'Bryan, leadership capabilities expanded through innovative approaches to team development. The implementation of Tony Robbins' "Power to Influence" program, combined with creative presentation strategies, transformed the sales team's effectiveness. The partnership with John O'Bryan exemplified how complementary skills and collaborative leadership could break the traditional "lone wolf" model of real estate sales, creating a more effective team-based structure.

Beyond technical and leadership innovations, the chapter illustrates the power of authentic community involvement through organizations like Junior Achievement, The Real Estate Forum, and the Toronto Board of Trade. These experiences proved that genuine engagement in meaningful initiatives builds stronger professional networks than traditional networking approaches.

The narrative reinforces the core theme of *The Consistency Effect*: that transformative success comes not from occasional grand slams but from the steady accumulation of singles and doubles: daily excellence, continuous learning, and meaningful relationships. Whether developing new systems, building teams, or creating industry networks, sustainable achievement grows from consistent effort rather than dramatic individual plays.

My life was awesome, and I was proud of all these successes. Little did I know this was all about to change and not in a good way.

Key Takeaways:

1. Career Foundations

- Entry-level positions can provide invaluable industry knowledge.

- Thorough understanding of fundamentals creates lasting advantages.

- Seemingly menial tasks can mask hidden opportunities for growth.

2. Innovation and Adaptation

- Embracing new technologies can transform traditional industries.

- Being an early adopter can create significant competitive advantages.

- Limited technical knowledge shouldn't prevent technological innovation.

3. **Mentorship Impact**

- Strong mentors can accelerate professional development.

- Open knowledge sharing creates organizational strength.

- Learning from industry leaders provides invaluable insights.

4. **Team Building and Culture**

- Collaborative approaches often outperform individual efforts.

- Creative presentation methods can transform team performance.

- Building trust through authenticity creates lasting relationships.

5. **Professional Growth**

- Success comes from consistent effort and continuous learning.

- Adaptability and willingness to embrace change are crucial.

- Building strong relationships creates lasting career opportunities.

6. Strategic Networking

- Authentic community involvement builds stronger networks than formal networking.

- Focus on giving rather than getting yields better results.

- Shared purpose creates lasting professional relationships.

These lessons demonstrate that while individual achievements matter, sustainable success comes from building strong foundations, embracing innovation, and fostering meaningful relationships through consistent effort and authentic engagement.

6th Inning

Getting Thrown Out of the Game: When Success Becomes a Liability

---

"Success is a lousy teacher. It seduces smart people into thinking they can't lose." — Bill Gates

---

Learning Objectives:

After reading this chapter, you will:

- Understand how success can sometimes create unexpected challenges

- Learn how to navigate corporate transitions and identity shifts

- Recognize the importance of maintaining independence from corporate identity

- Understand the challenges and opportunities in industry transitions

- Learn to adapt skills across different business sectors

- Recognize patterns in career setbacks and recoveries

- Understand how personal challenges impact professional life

- Learn to balance professional obligations with personal crises

In baseball, even the strongest teams can face unexpected challenges. Sometimes, these challenges come not from competitors but from within their own organization. My story took such a turn, demonstrating how success can sometimes create unforeseen complications.

The Compensation Curveball

As the market dynamics drove up rents, sales professionals' incomes naturally increased through commission structures. As managers, John and I saw our maintained transparency about our compensation, and we deliberately benchmarked ourselves against top salespeople to ensure we weren't out earning them. Our compensation typically ranked in the top third to two-thirds of the company's top 10 earners.

However, senior management grew increasingly uncomfortable with branch management compensation levels across the company. The original structure, 4% of gross revenue and 17% of profit, was revised to 2% of the top line and 30% of profit. This adjustment was designed to focus management on bottom-line results. However, it effectively reduced management compensation for consistent rather than spectacular performance levels.

The Backfire

What senior management hadn't anticipated was how the improvements John and I had implemented would affect this new formula. After the painful markets of the early '90s, the initiatives we had launched drove revenue levels to unprecedented levels, while costs remained relatively stable. This dream scenario led to exponential profit growth in the largest market in Canada. Instead of reducing or stabilizing our compensation as intended, the new focus on profit margin increased it significantly, creating embarrassment for senior management.

Their solution? A far more drastic compensation cut introduced and implemented after the new compensation year had already begun. Despite any attempts to negotiate, it was a very much "take it or leave it" situation. This forced us to seek legal counsel, who advised that we were effectively being constructively dismissed.

Constructive dismissal occurs when an employer fundamentally changes essential terms of employment without the employee's agreement or without appropriate notice, effectively forcing them to resign. Key elements might include a significant reduction in compensation, a major change in duties or responsibilities, or other employment terms. The key point is that these changes are so substantial that they breach the employment contract, making continued employment untenable. When this occurs, the employee can treat the employment relationship as terminated and may be entitled to severance as if they had been formally fired. This is exactly what happened in this case.

High-Stakes Showdown

When corporate politics reached a boiling point, I witnessed something extraordinary – a display of loyalty and integrity that would shape my understanding of true partnership forever. While senior management played hardball with our compensation, assuming we'd never risk leaving, they failed to account for the strength of the partnership John and I had.

What unfolded next still amazes me decades later. In the eyes of senior management, John was salvageable while I was expendable. He could have easily carved out his own path, securing his position without any need to actively work against me; simply stepping aside would have sufficed. Instead, John demonstrated an unwavering loyalty that redefined my understanding of professional relationships.

Senior management held numerous meetings with John, trying to persuade him to stay on in the new regime. I felt increasingly uncomfortable while this was happening, but in every instance, John kept me fully up to speed on the nature of the discussions and his unrelenting loyalty to our partnership. I felt duty bound to my principles. I did not want to stay in an organization that was going to treat me so cavalierly. On the other hand, I was in my late thirties and had spent the last 18 years at this company. It was a scary time for me.

In a move that spoke volumes about his character, John tied our interests together, refusing senior management's attempts to divide us. His stance wasn't just about partnership; it was about principles. When we were ultimately asked to "not return to the company's offices," a polite corporate euphemism for termination, we faced it together. The subsequent two-year legal battle, though resolved in our favor, felt hollow compared to the lesson in integrity I'd witnessed.

John's display of loyalty transcended typical professional relationships. It became my gold standard for leadership and partnership, influencing how I approach both business and personal relationships to this day. His mentorship extended far beyond traditional business lessons – it was a masterclass in ethics, leadership, and the power of genuine partnership and, ultimately, friendship – a friendship that has now lasted longer than the time we worked together.

Looking back, I realize John wasn't just a colleague or mentor. He was a transformative force who elevated everyone around him. His influence shaped not only our immediate team but the entire organizational culture. They say people enter your life for a reason, a season, or a lifetime. What began as a professional partnership with John evolved into a lifelong friendship, teaching me that true success isn't measured solely by corporate achievements but by the strength and quality of the relationships we build along the way.

When, in later years I asked John about why he acted in the way he did, his answer was disarmingly simple. He said partnerships are about a commitment to a shared goal. To abandon your partner was an act of betrayal, which probably accounts for his 50-year marriage and long list of lifelong friends. He also added, very perceptively, that even if he had been tempted to remain with his compensation intact, then his own day of reckoning would have merely been a matter of when and not if. His basic credo was that life presents you with a myriad of opportunities but only one reputation.

His impact continues to resonate, serving as a testament to the enduring power of mentorship and friendship in shaping not just careers, but lives. It's a reminder that the most valuable lessons often transcend the boardroom, teaching us not just how to succeed in business, but how to thrive in the game of life itself.

The Hidden Impact

What I didn't recognize at the time was the existential impact this situation would have on me personally. Like a career-changing injury in sports, this experience would fundamentally alter my perspective on corporate loyalty, success metrics, and personal identity. The lesson wasn't just about compensation structures or corporate politics. It was about understanding that success can sometimes create its own unique set of challenges.

A Job for Life or a Lifetime of Employment: A New Ball Game

The landscape of career evolution has transformed dramatically. Once, lifelong employment with a single company was common, offering stability and a clear progression path. Today's professionals are more like free agents, managing their careers independently and accumulating skills and experiences across various "leagues" and "positions." This shift reflects broader changes in the economic landscape and evolving attitudes towards career success. My departure from LePage in the late 1990s came during this transition period, as the workplace was evolving from long-term employment to career mobility.

The Aftermath: Rebuilding an Identity and my Support Systems

As mentioned in the last chapter, about mid-way through my journey at LePage, I was invited to join the board of directors of a local Junior Achievement chapter in the Greater Toronto Area. Junior Achievement's mission was to help youth prepare for success in the business world. At the time, I had been with LePage for about eight years and was very happy. Junior Achievement's curriculum was to teach young adults that they would likely have 3 to 5 different jobs in 2 to 3 different industries. I always saw myself as an exception to that rule, believing I would stay with LePage for a very long time.

What followed my departure from LePage was more than just a career transition – it was an existential earthquake that shook the very foundation of my identity. Like the ivy on Wrigley Field's walls, my sense of self had become deeply entwined with my corporate role. When that role vanished, it wasn't just a job loss; it was as if someone had erased my name from the lineup of life. This feeling eerily echoed my earlier experience leaving the music industry, but with an even deeper impact given the years invested.

I hadn't realized how completely my life had become encased in a corporate cocoon. My social circle was predominantly work-related – colleagues, clients, and industry contacts formed the core of my daily interactions. Business lunches, corporate events, and industry functions weren't just work obligations; they were my primary social outlets. Even my weekends were typically with work associates, making the line between professional and personal life virtually nonexistent.

The technological aspects of this separation hit particularly hard. My entire digital life was housed in corporate systems, from my email to my contacts database. At that time, it was usual for people to have their own digital identity. My laptop, phone, and other devices were company property, requiring me to rebuild my technological infrastructure from scratch. It was like being a modern professional suddenly transported back to the digital stone age. The contact information for thousands of professional relationships, built over decades, remained locked in corporate databases, requiring a painstaking reconstruction effort. This period of upheaval forced me to confront uncomfortable questions about who I was beyond my professional role. I had spent years building a personal brand so closely aligned with my corporate identity that separating the two felt like trying to unscramble an egg. I was like a star player who'd not only lost his team but had to question whether he was still a player at all. But life-changing moments have a way of clearing your vision, much like how a rain delay can provide clarity during a crucial game. This forced pause made me realize I'd been operating under an outdated playbook. The modern business world wasn't about lifetime contracts with a single team; it was about adaptability, versatility, and personal brand independence.

This realization led to a fundamental shift in my approach to career and identity. Instead of seeking another permanent home team, I embraced the role of a free agent. This meant viewing my career not as a single, continuous game, but as a series of seasons, each offering opportunities to apply my skills in new ways and learn from different organizations.

Building Independence

I began constructing an independent professional identity:

- Creating personal email and contact management systems

- Establishing my own professional network separate from any employer

- Developing a personal brand that transcended any single organization

- Building relationships that weren't dependent on work or corporate affiliations

The Junior Achievement Prophecy

Those early mentors at Junior Achievement, who predicted careers would span multiple companies and industries, had been more prescient than I'd realized. Their wisdom about career flexibility and adaptability now became my guiding principle.

This transformation wasn't just about professional reinvention; it was about fundamental personal growth. I learned that true career security doesn't come from organizational attachment but from maintaining adaptability, continuing to learn, and building genuine relationships that transcend corporate boundaries.

The experience taught me that in the modern business world, you need to be your own team owner while playing as a free agent – managing your brand, skills, and relationships independently of any single organization. It's about being ready to step up to the plate in any stadium, wearing any jersey, while maintaining your unique identity and value proposition.

Now as an executive coach, I can see clearly when people are travelling down this road, and I can at least caution them about the perils of too tightly intertwining their personal and professional identity.

A Different Approach: Swinging in Tech with a Real Estate Playbook

My career setback from LePage prompted me to re-evaluate my approach and consider my next move. Would I return to the same industry, or was it time for a change? I decided to switch fields entirely, moving from commercial real estate to the tech world.

However, I quickly learned that deciding to change industries doesn't make it happen automatically. Transitioning between sectors in business is incredibly challenging. It's comparable to a seasoned player deciding to switch sports entirely, a feat that even legendary athletes have found daunting. Take Michael Jordan, for instance, whose attempt to transition from basketball to baseball demonstrated just how difficult such a change can be, even for someone at the top of their game.

This transition and subsequent desire to change industries took place in the late 1990s, when commercialization of the internet had set the stage for the dot-com boom. Advances in technology made personal computers more affordable and accessible, while the proliferation of internet service providers expanded connectivity. The World Wide Web introduced new possibilities for communication, commerce, and information sharing which ignited public interest and entrepreneurial ambition.

Investors, captivated by the transformative potential of the internet, poured capital into start-ups with untested business models. Venture capital firms aggressively funded internet companies, often valuing them based on projected future growth rather than current profitability. Stock markets, particularly the NASDAQ Composite index, saw unprecedented surges as initial public offerings (IPOs) of dot-com companies attracted enthusiastic participation from both institutional and retail investors.

So, while I was on my journey to try to find my next opportunity, I got a call from someone I met in commercial real estate. He was a serial entrepreneur who had started a company, grown it exponentially and had a successful commercial exit. Based on all that was going on with the Internet, he had a new idea. StarPages was an online directory, particularly for small and medium size companies, who did not have a web presence. For a subscription fee, a company would get a webpage and a listing in the StarPages online directories. This was a fast and affordable way for small businesses to get online. Remember, this was before Google when the likes of Netscape, Microsoft Internet Explorer, and Mosaic were the browsers of choice?

At the time the news was buzzing with start-ups who prioritized rapid expansion to capture market share, adhering to the mantra "get big fast." Profit margins and sustainable revenue models were frequently overlooked. Traditional financial metrics were often disregarded. Companies with minimal earnings (or none at all), achieved multi-billion-dollar market capitalizations based on optimistic forecasts and speculative fervour. It sounded like the perfect way to repatriate my former glory. A big swing for the fences to make millions – like everyone else seemed to be doing. So, I dove in headfirst not just joining the company but investing a significant amount of my own money as a shareholder.

I had just left a very successful organization where I had a large staff of people doing things for me. A start-up is a very different environment. While I am very self-sufficient, the primary purpose of the company was to hire legions of salespeople to go door-to-door to small businesses to sell advertising. This was a very different process with very different people. Instead of negotiating multi-million-dollar real estate deals, I was now working with salespeople selling small-scale internet advertising. In addition, these were early days of the internet, and while many people had computers, the power and the speed of the internet was still emerging. I remember going on a sales call and talking to one prospective customer who asked how his customers would find him on the internet. When we opened our computer and went online, he clocked it at a minute or two. By contrast, he took out the yellow pages and found his ad in seconds. We were selling a future which had not arrived yet.

Also, I had taken on this executive role, based purely on full commission. Given that I had just come off my best year and a seven-figure compensation, I did not need a paycheck, I wanted a big score. But given our lacklustre sales, the compensation did not amount to very much. I quickly realized that this situation was not for me, but with a start-up, your shares are locked up until there is a capital event. While I was anxious that my investment may be in jeopardy, I saw no other path than to transition to a pure shareholder and hope for the best.

What did I learn from this experience? First and foremost, I learned that start-ups are not for everyone. I was much more a manager of ongoing operations. So, while I was considering my next move, I decided to take a role as a salesperson in commercial real estate. After all, this was something I understood. Sales would give me a tremendous amount of freedom to pursue other endeavours and allow me to make some money in the interim. I joined Colliers International, which was one of LePage's major competitors. The team at Colliers were extremely welcoming. One of the things I decided right off the bat was that I would never do a deal by myself. Rather, I would take the opportunity to invite other colleagues into every transaction with me. This is partly selfish, as I knew they would be counted on to do most of the work and that it would likely trigger reciprocity for me to be brought into other transactions. This strategy worked perfectly, and a number of opportunities came my way very early on.

Along the way, I was approached by a couple of ambitious MBA students I had met while I was a guest lecturer at York University. They were brewing an idea that struck a chord with me. The students were energetic, smart, and eager to solve a problem that had been plaguing Canadian consumers. It was the late 1990s, and back then, shopping online from U.S. retailers wasn't the smooth experience that we take for granted today – especially if you were living in Canada.

They explained that Canadian shoppers constantly faced hurdles when buying from U.S. websites. Prices were listed in U.S. dollars, making it hard to know the real cost after converting currency. Duties and taxes were often a surprise, and delivery times of over a week were standard. Returns? Forget about it. The process was complicated, and you'd often have to ship products right back across the border. And then there was customer service, which was rarely prepared to help Canadian buyers, let alone those who spoke French. These issues led many Canadian consumers to abandon their purchases in frustration.

The students envisioned e-Tech Direct as the solution to these issues. Their idea was to launch a Direct e-Commerce Solution in Canada that would change the game for cross-border shopping. They planned to establish fulfillment centers in Canada, cutting delivery times down to just 24 to 48 hours, and display prices in Canadian dollars – no more guessing what the total bill would be. Duties, taxes, packaging, labeling – all of it would be handled seamlessly, in compliance with Canadian regulations.

They even thought about the little things that made a big difference. Customer service would be available 24/7, in both English and French, making sure nobody felt left out or frustrated. They planned to create a portal called buyUSAnow.com, which would act as an aggregator of well-known U.S. brands, giving Canadians a smooth way to access these products without the typical headaches. Returns would be simplified too, with local centers to handle them and shipping costs covered.

Now this was a big vision. One I wanted to be a part of. The best part, their expectation was that they would raise a lot of money like a lot of other people and be able to build a large dynamic organization quickly. They wanted me to be one of their executives.

While this was happening, StarPages, the other start-up I had invested in, completed a reverse takeover of a shell company listed on the Vancouver venture exchange. This was an inexpensive way for a company to go public. A privately held company would take over a publicly traded company and become instantly listed. Once this happened, the share price increased rapidly, as was the case with any company with a .com in its name, and my shares were worth an astronomical $8 million.

Although I never wholeheartedly believed that the shares would be worth that much money, I secretly hope that they would. Nonetheless, with that in the background I invested in e-Tech.

The Bubble Bursts

In March 2000, skepticism about the viability of many dot-com companies led to a sharp decline in stock prices. An overabundance of companies vying for the same market segments diluted profitability, and as quarterly reports revealed consistent losses, confidence waned. At the same time, interest rate hikes and concerns about inflation prompted a re-evaluation of high-risk investments. The NASDAQ Composite index plummeted from its peak of over 5,000 in March 2000 to around 1,100 by October 2002. Countless companies declared bankruptcy, and trillions of dollars in market value evaporated.

My investment in StarPages? I was able to get out with my initial investment before it ceased operation. I was not so lucky with e-Tech where all the shareholders lost their investments.

Aftermath and Legacy

The dot-com boom of the late 1990s was a transformative period that reshaped the global economy and the technological landscape. Companies like Amazon and eBay not only survived but flourished, leveraging the lessons learned to build resilient, diversified businesses. While it ended in a significant market correction, the era's innovations and experiences laid the groundwork for the digital advancements that followed. It remains a pivotal chapter in the history of the internet, offering valuable insights into the interplay between technology, economics, and human behavior.

Monday Morning Coach: You Always Win in Retrospect

Looking back at my experiences with StarPages and e-Tech through the lens of the GRAND SLAM framework, I can see where I hit and where I missed:

Great Idea: I could see the values in both ventures. StarPages aimed to solve a real problem for small businesses, and e-Tech addressed genuine pain points for Canadian online shoppers. But I realize now that I was a bit ahead of the curve. The market wasn't quite ready. Internet speeds were still slow, and customers were skeptical.

Resilience: While I showed resilience in my overall career by bouncing back from these setbacks, I didn't apply enough resilience within these ventures. When challenges arose, we couldn't adapt quickly enough to keep the businesses afloat.

Ambition: My ambition served me well in taking the leap into tech, but I see now that it was misdirected. I was too focused on the potential financial windfall and not enough on building sustainable businesses.

Network: My network opened doors, connecting me with these opportunities. However, I didn't have the right network in the tech industry to provide the expertise and support I needed to navigate these unfamiliar industries and the perils of start-ups.

Discipline: This is where I really dropped the ball. I didn't apply the same disciplined approach I'd used in real estate. We were too caught up in the "get big fast" mentality of the time.

Skill: I overestimated how well my real estate skills would translate to tech start-ups. I lacked the industry-specific experience we needed, and I didn't do enough to fill that gap.

Luck: Initially, luck was on my side with the timing of the dot-com boom. But when the bubble burst, it turned against me hard and fast.

Action: I took decisive action in joining and investing in these ventures, which I'm proud of. But the actions were blinded by the prospect of a grand slam.

Mentors: This is a glaring omission in my approach. I didn't seek out mentors or experienced advisors in the tech industry. Their guidance could have been invaluable in helping us navigate this unfamiliar territory.

In hindsight, I see that while I had some elements working in my favor, like a Great Idea and plenty of Ambition, I was missing crucial pieces of the puzzle. I lacked the right Skills for the tech industry, didn't apply enough Discipline in building the businesses, and failed to seek out proper Mentorship. When Luck turned against me with the dot-com crash, it was a tough lesson, but it taught me the importance of having all elements of GRAND SLAM in place for sustainable success.

Undeterred, I continued my journey looking for that next opportunity in tech. This time I wanted a real company, with real products and services that had momentum. This next opportunity came to me from one of my colleagues at Colliers International, Ian Gragtsmans. Ian and I worked together on a number of deals and he came to appreciate my managerial capabilities. He introduced me to one of his clients, named Paul Goldman, who had a Moneyball mindset and saw value in drafting players from other sports. I was hired as President of Arqana Technologies, an IT Systems Integration Company. (I know, nice entry-level job. I got lucky).

In this new tech league, I might not have known a computer rack from a fridge (Paul's quote), but subject matter expertise wasn't the company's primary problem. Like many small companies, it had grown to the point where it got itself tied up in organizational knots. This is where my skills and capabilities in playing on a bigger team and in a different league came into play. My approach was different from Arqana's typical competitors. My commercial real estate experience had me pitching to the C-suite while most tech folks were talking to the technology-level folks.

We embarked on a comprehensive overhaul of the company's operations, implementing a wide array of new procedures and protocols. Our goal was to create a well-oiled machine, where every process was clearly defined and efficiently executed. This involved countless hours of analysis, planning, and implementation, often requiring us to rethink long-standing practices and challenge the status quo.

Simultaneously, we turned our attention to the organizational structure. We meticulously reviewed every role and department, identifying redundancies and inefficiencies. Through careful restructuring, we streamlined the organization chart, creating clear lines of responsibility and communication. This leaner, more agile structure allowed for faster decision-making and improved responsiveness to market changes.

Our efforts didn't stop at internal improvements. We also focused on enhancing our market position, refining our product offerings, and strengthening our client relationships. This holistic approach to business transformation paid off in ways we couldn't have initially imagined.

The culmination of these efforts was the successful sale of the company to TELUS Communications. The deal was struck at a price that exceeded our most optimistic projections, representing a significant return on investment for all stakeholders involved.

From a personal standpoint, this experience proved to be a pivotal moment in my career. It demonstrated my ability to lead a company through a significant transformation and ultimately to a successful exit. While the financial rewards were certainly welcome, the real value lay in the skills I developed and the credibility I gained in the business world. This experience opened new opportunities and set the stage for the next phase of my career, allowing me to take on even more challenging roles in the future.

Unexpected Runs: Transforming Challenges into Career Victories

My next at-bat was with TELUS Communications, but the path there wasn't a straight line. After successfully integrating Arqana into TELUS – a challenge complicated by the fact that none of our team were TELUS employees nor did we have deep knowledge of the organization – an unexpected opportunity emerged. A senior manager, wanting to shift me from day-to-day operations of the newly integrated division, put my name forward for a company-wide cost-cutting initiative.

This led to a pivotal meeting with Andrew Turner, a British expatriate who had worked with CEO Darren Entwistle at Cable and Wireless in the UK. Darren had brought Andrew over to assist with TELUS's transformation, trusting his capabilities from their shared history. Andrew was impressed enough with my work to champion me to Darren, effectively launching my role as TELUS' "Fix-it Guy."

What started as a short-term contract evolved into a series of clutch performances that caught

Darren's attention. This led to opportunities to manage underperforming divisions, despite my limited experience in these areas. Through careful assessment and strategic planning, I consistently charted paths to success. I found myself managing more turnarounds than a ballet dancer.

Through managing this many projects I learned a valuable lesson: Most people know the right play to make, but they're often too afraid of striking out to swing. In response, I became a confidence coach, encouraging my team to take bold action while assuring them I would accept responsibility for any setbacks. This approach was revolutionary; it removed the fear of failure that had been holding them back. Once they felt truly supported, their performance soared, creating a powerful momentum that transformed our entire team. For me it was just the consistency of doing what I would normally do, but it was a confidence building exercise to see it being successful in a new industry.

The journey also brought unexpected financial rewards. In the early years at TELUS, my compensation from Arqana wasn't aligned with TELUS' policy. I accepted a rearranged compensation package that included stock options. Although skeptical at first, the options ended up being worth significantly more than my previous bonuses, thanks to a major restructuring and favorable market conditions. It just goes to show, sometimes when you think you're being traded, you're being called up to the majors – a career and financial double.

A Forced Timeout: When Life Throws a Wild Ball

Life has a way of throwing challenges at us when we least expect them, and sometimes these challenges seem insurmountable.

I had been married to my wife, Laurie, for 16 years. We had been together for a few years before that, building a life and a family with our two beautiful boys, aged 11 and 15. We had enjoyed a certain level of success and were beginning to reap the rewards of our hard work.

In the fall of 2003, Laurie noticed some dry skin on her scalp. What seemed like a routine visit to the doctor turned into a life-altering moment when the biopsy revealed malignant melanoma.

Laurie was one of nine children, the third youngest. Her parents were in their 80s and remarkably healthy for their age. She lived a comparatively healthy lifestyle, certainly healthier than mine, and was a beloved daughter, mother, friend, and wife. I expected if anyone was going to get sick it would have been me.

The diagnosis set in motion a relentless sequence of doctors' appointments, operations, radiation, chemotherapy, and an endless search for best practices across the globe. We considered any possibility of success, no matter how remote.

Melanoma is one of the most insidious forms of cancer. Although it's a form of skin cancer, it metastasizes and spreads rapidly. Time became our greatest adversary.

I held a strong belief that faith and hope were powerful healers. Stories of people making miraculous recoveries from cancer were inspiring, and I believed that maintaining hope in treatment and survival was crucial.

I saw my primary role as being that faith provider, particularly for my wife. I also had to help my two tween-aged sons understand the gravity of the situation while maintaining unwavering hope that they would have their mother for a lifetime. It was a challenging balance between optimism and realism.

Throughout this time, I faced numerous personal and professional conflicts. I held a senior position with many commitments. These were decisions I hadn't faced before. Previously, I had always been able to find appropriate compromises, but now, there was no one who needed my unwavering support more than my wife and boys. My affirmation became that I did not want to have a single regret.

As treatments yielded minimal results and the cancer spread to Laurie's lungs and brain, I kept focusing on what was next – the next treatment, the next expert we could engage.

Telling my sons that the possibility of their mother passing away had become an eventuality was, without a doubt, the hardest thing I've ever had to do.

In the early summer of 2005, Anne Lorraine (Laurie) Bingham Henderson passed away from her illness.

Death brings sadness, regardless of how it comes. When it comes quickly, it's a shock, and mourning starts immediately. When it comes after a long, protracted, and painful illness, the mourning begins before death, and while there is some relief that the suffering is over, the mourning continues thereafter.

This was the most existential challenge I had ever faced. The days following Laurie's funeral were a stark reminder of how quickly the world moves on, even when your own has been shattered. The flood of support that had buoyed us through her illness and the immediate aftermath of her passing began to recede, leaving me standing alone on an unfamiliar shore. I found myself in a role I had never anticipated, a single father to two grieving boys, trying to navigate a life that no longer resembled the one we had planned.

In those early days, I grappled with an overwhelming sense of pressure. There was a constant, nagging feeling that I needed to have all the answers, to make immediate decisions about our future, to somehow fill the enormous void left by Laurie's absence. I fixated on what we had lost: not just Laurie herself, but the future we had envisioned together, the milestones we would never share, the dreams that had evaporated like morning mist.

The weight of these expectations was crushing. I found myself paralyzed by the magnitude of the decisions before me. What was the right path forward? How could I possibly make choices that would affect my boys' lives so profoundly? The questions seemed endless, and the answers frustratingly elusive.

It was during this period of intense introspection and struggle that I had a realization, one that would become a guiding principle in the months and years to come. I concluded that trying to figure everything out at once, to have a grand plan for our future, was not only impossible but potentially harmful. Instead, I decided to focus on taking things one day at a time.

This approach – putting one foot in front of the other and to keep moving – became my mantra. It was about embracing the present moment, dealing with the challenges of each day as they came, rather than becoming overwhelmed by an uncertain future. This shift in perspective was transformative. It gave me permission to take things slowly, to give ourselves time to grieve and adjust.

This reframing wasn't about diminishing our loss or pretending that everything was fine. Rather, it was about finding a balance: acknowledging our grief while also recognizing the beauty and value that remained in our lives. It was about honoring Laurie's memory by living fully and appreciating the gifts she had left us.

This experience, as painful and challenging as it was, showed me that even in our darkest moments, there is hope. These lessons have made me a more empathetic leader, a more present father, and a more resilient individual.

There is no doubt that as we move to build consistency in our life, we cannot always control what happens to us, but we can control how we respond. And sometimes, the most powerful response is simply to keep moving forward, one step at a time.

Bottom of the 6th Inning

This inning explores the paradoxical nature of success and its unforeseen consequences. Through personal experiences ranging from corporate politics to personal tragedy, we see how life's curveballs can fundamentally alter our path. The chapter demonstrates that true success isn't just about professional achievements but about maintaining integrity, building genuine relationships, and adapting to change.

Whether facing corporate challenges or personal loss, the key lies in taking things one day at a time while maintaining a forward focus. The transformation from company man to free agent reflects broader changes in the business world, highlighting the importance of building an independent professional identity and maintaining adaptability in modern careers.

Navigating your own professional setback? Transform challenges into opportunities with structured executive coaching support. Book a confidential consultation at consistency-edge.com.

Key Takeaways:

1. Success Management

- Corporate success can sometimes create unexpected challenges.

- Success metrics need to align with organizational goals.

- Building independent professional identity is crucial.

- Maintain awareness of changing business landscapes.

2. Professional Relationships

- True partnerships transcend corporate boundaries.

- Loyalty and integrity matter more than short-term gains.

- Professional networks should extend beyond current employer.

- Build relationships that survive organizational changes.

3. Career Evolution

- The concept of lifetime employment has transformed.

- Career security comes from adaptability, not stability.

- Personal brand should transcend any single organization.

- Maintain independence in professional identity.

4. Personal Resilience

- Major life changes require flexibility and patience.

- Taking things "one day at a time" can be a powerful strategy.

- Balance between professional success and personal life is crucial.

- Control lies in how we respond to challenges, not the challenges themselves.

5. Identity Management

- Professional identity should be separate from corporate role.

- Build personal infrastructure independent of employer.

- Maintain relationships beyond corporate boundaries.

- Create support systems that transcend work environment

Top of the 7th Inning:

"Passion is energy. Feel the power that comes from focusing on what excites you." — Oprah Winfrey

---

Learning Objectives:

After reading this chapter, you will:

- Understand the fundamental principles of effective coaching and being coachable

- Master the Socratic method of leadership through questioning.

- Learn to balance different leadership philosophies

- Develop effective delegation skills

- Understand how to build confidence in others

- Learn to transition from individual contributor to leader

- Master the art of clear communication in leadership

When Past Passions Meet Present Purpose

After the profound personal challenges of losing Laurie, my career at TELUS took an unexpected turn that brought my past and present together in an unexpected way. In a delightful twist of fate, my abandoned rock star dreams found a new stage through the TELUS corporate band, started by Executive Vice President Joe Grech. When I mentioned my drumming background, his immediate response – "Great, we need a drummer" – opened the door to an experience that blended my former passion with my current life.

What began as a modest corporate initiative evolved into something far more significant. During a period of labor disruption, CEO Darren Entwistle transformed the band into a morale-boosting force, sending us on tour to various TELUS offices across Canada. We went on to perform for thousands of employees at Christmas parties and corporate events, complete with professional sound systems, technicians, and even corporate jet travel.

The pinnacle came when we opened for the renowned Canadian band Great Big Sea at a

TELUS-sponsored event. It was the closest I'd come to my original rock star dreams, albeit in a completely unexpected context. This experience taught me that no passion is ever wasted – the dreams we nurture, even those we think we've left behind, often find their way back to us in surprising and meaningful ways. When we remain open to possibility and continue growing, life has a way of weaving our past experiences into the fabric of our present success.

Big Format Learnings

Before coming to TELUS, the largest company I ever worked for was a LePage. By comparison, TELUS was five times bigger with more than 40,000 people and $9 billion of revenue at the time. With that size and scale came an abundance of very smart people and a considerable amount of process. In comparison to the smaller, more agile companies where I recently worked, where a lack of process was their Achilles heel, in an organization like TELUS, an excessive amount of arguably unnecessary process contributed to bureaucracy.

With all the various roles I had, I spent the most time on streamlining existing processes. Notwithstanding, many of the processes had strong reasons for being and provided me with a graduate level education in the art of managing large groups of people and processes.

Of all the concepts I gained through TELUS, the one that stands out the most is people performance management. What I learned had a dramatic effect on my people management skills. It also gave me the philosophy and tools that I took viral, carrying it to various other organizations. But before we get to TELUS' specific approach, I would like to explore the popular paradigm of people performance management, which continues in many corporations today.

The Power of Effective People Management: Beyond the Sandwich

In the early days of modern management, feedback often followed what Mary Kay Ash popularized as the "sandwich method," delivering criticism nestled between two layers of praise, like a bitter filling between sweet bread. While well-intentioned, the sandwich approach often left employees confused about the real message and skeptical about the authenticity of the praise.

Think about it, if every piece of constructive feedback comes wrapped in compliments, employees quickly learn to brace for criticism whenever they receive praise. Furthermore, employees come prepared with a list of activities that support their claim of excellent performance. The sandwich method, despite its good intentions, can create a culture of anxiety and mistrust, where genuine praise becomes indistinguishable from diplomatic cushioning.

Moreover, this approach often dilutes the impact of both positive and negative feedback. The praise can seem insincere–- mere packaging for the real message – while the constructive criticism might lose its urgency when buried between compliments. It's like trying to have a serious conversation about batting technique while simultaneously praising the player's uniform and their excellent dugout etiquette.

Balanced Scorecard: A Better Way to Keep Score

Enter the Balanced Scorecard approach, a shift in how we think about and measure performance. This system moves away from the subjective, often anxiety-inducing feedback sessions of the past toward a more comprehensive, objective, and empowering method of performance management. It focuses on creating clarity and alignment between individual performance and organizational goals. It's like having a clear scoreboard where everyone knows exactly how points are earned and what constitutes a win. This is the promise of the Balanced Scorecard approach which I was introduced to at TELUS.

Here's how it works:

1. Clear Objectives: Distill each role down to 3-7 key objectives that truly matter to the organization.

2. SMART Goal Setting: Make the goals specific, measurable, actionable, relevant, and time bound.

3. Define Goals: For each objective, define a range of outcomes from "unacceptable" to "dramatically exceeds expectations."

4. Numerical Clarity: Assign scores (1-5) to each performance level, with 3 representing "meets expectations."

5. Redefining "Average": Challenge the notion that 3 out of 5 is mediocre. Meeting expectations should be celebrated!

6. Aligned Compensation: Tie variable-pay directly to scorecard performance, creating a clear link between results and rewards.

7. Stretch Goals: Set ambitious yet achievable targets for "exceeds" and "dramatically exceeds"

categories, ensuring these wins significantly benefit the organization.

Redefining Success: The Power of Clear Metrics

The Balanced Scorecard's effectiveness hinges on two crucial elements that transform traditional performance evaluation:

Reimagining the Rating Scale

Traditional academic scoring has conditioned us to view a 3 out of 5 as mediocre, equivalent to a C grade or 60%. The Balanced Scorecard fundamentally reshapes this perception. In this system:

3 = Meets Expectations (Solid Performance)
4 = Exceeds Expectations (Superior Performance)
5 = Dramatically Exceeds Expectations (Exceptional Performance)
2 = Needs Work (Below Standard)
1 = Unacceptable (Significant Improvement Required)

This recalibration is crucial because it recognizes that meeting all job requirements (a "3") is actually a strong performance worthy of respect. It's not a middle-ground compromise but rather a benchmark of professional competence.

Defining Clear Success Criteria

The second vital component is establishing detailed, specific criteria for each performance level. This means clearly outlining what behaviors, achievements, and outcomes correspond to each rating. For example:

Level 3 (Meets Expectations) might include:

- Consistently meeting deadlines

- Achieving target metrics

- Following standard procedures effectively

Level 4 (Exceeds Expectations) could involve:

- Innovating process improvements

- Mentoring colleagues

- Exceeding targets by defined percentages

Level 5 (Dramatically Exceeds) might require:

- Creating transformative solutions

- Leading major initiatives

- Achieving breakthrough results

By adding as much detailed definition to each of the performance levels, employees know exactly how to achieve each level, making performance management more objective and actionable.

Transforming Performance Through Clear Expectations

When employees understand exactly what excellence looks like, it changes the entire dynamic of performance management.This system creates several powerful advantages:

Motivation Through Clarity

- Employees can clearly see their path to improvement
- Success becomes a series of defined, achievable steps
- The mystery of "what it takes to get ahead" disappears
- Performance goals become tangible rather than abstract

Creating a Culture of Achievement

Instead of fostering anxiety about being "average," this system:

- Celebrates consistent, reliable performance (Level 3)

- Provides clear targets for those aspiring to excel (Levels 4 and 5)

- Removes the stigma from areas needing improvement (Level 2)

- Creates healthy competition based on clear metrics

Empowering Development Conversations

This framework transforms performance discussions from subjective evaluations into strategic planning sessions:

- Managers can point to specific, observable behaviors

- Employees can self-assess against clear criteria

- Development plans become more focused and actionable

- Feedback becomes more objective and less personal

Aligning Compensation with Performance

The system can create a clear link between performance and rewards:

- Variable pay tied directly to achievement levels. In the case of TELUS, variable compensation at target was paid out for performance of 3.

- Extra recognition and variable compensation for truly exceptional performance (Levels 4 and 5)

- Less variable compensation for level 2 and minimal to no variable compensation for Level 1 performance.

- Clear justification for compensation decisions

- Transparent path to increased earnings

Building Your "Magic Makers"

This approach naturally identifies and nurtures top talent:

1. Consistent Level 4 and 5 performers were identified

2. High performers can be fast-tracked for development

3. Investment in top talent becomes more targeted (i.e. extra money spent on developing exceptional performers for their next role)

4. Success becomes self-reinforcing

The Ripple Effect

As this system takes hold, it creates positive organizational change:

- Performance expectations become clearer across the organization

- Team members understand how they contribute to overall success

- Goals are cascaded down from the highest levels

- Managers become better coaches and mentors

- The organization develops a stronger performance culture

By moving beyond outdated methods like the "sandwich approach," we open the door to a more engaged, motivated, and high-performing workforce. This isn't just about managing people – it's about unleashing their full potential and driving your organization to new heights.

Want help implementing this performance management framework?

Many of my coaching clients have transformed their leadership using this strategy. I have created a comprehensive Performance Management Implementation Kit that includes:

1. System Implementation Guide

2. System Operation Guide and a

3. Performance Management (Excel) Workbook

Download your kit at www.consistency-edge.com/ pages/shop

While this comprehensive suite of tools enables leaders to independently design and implement an effective performance management system, experience shows that guided implementation often accelerates success and prevents common pitfalls.

For those seeking additional support, I offer a structured implementation program that combine these tools with expert guidance, leadership coaching, and proven change management strategies. Whether you choose self-implementation or a guided approach, my goal is to help you build a performance-driven culture that drives organizational success.

To explore how we can support your performance management journey, visit consistency-edge.com to learn more about our guided implementation options and Leadership Coaching.

Life's Transitions: From Professional to Personal Growth

While mastering the art of people management shaped my professional life, a deeply personal journey was unfolding in parallel. Just as I learned that effective leadership requires moving beyond traditional approaches, life taught me that personal growth often demands embracing unexpected changes and opportunities.

A New Beginning

The journey from loss to meeting a new love is rarely straightforward, and my experience was no exception. After Laurie's passing, I found myself grappling with dual challenges: concern for my boys' well-being and the profound question of my own identity. Just as my professional identity was deeply entwined with my role at LePage, my personal identity was fundamentally linked to being Laurie's husband.

The Question of Moving Forward

The guilt that accompanies thoughts of dating after losing a spouse is rarely discussed but intensely felt. How long should one wait? What's appropriate? What will others think?

It was Reverend Peter Holmes, a family friend, who offered perspective that proved both comforting and prophetic: "Of all my parishioners who have become widows or widowers, those that were happily married married again." His words suggested that experience with a loving partnership makes one more likely to seek it again, not less.

My introduction to Tanya Dorbyk came during my time at Arqana, where she stood out as one of the company's top salespeople. What caught my attention wasn't just her sales success, but her remarkable ability to bridge the traditional divide between sales and professional services teams, a gap that often-plagued technology companies. The running joke in the industry was that salespeople would sell solutions that the technical teams couldn't deliver, while the technical team would design solutions clients couldn't afford. Tanya, however, had a unique gift for bringing these disparate groups together, inspiring professional services teams to go above and beyond for her and her clients.

When the opportunity arose to appoint new sales leadership, Tanya was my immediate choice, despite her initial skepticism. Her response – looking at me as if I had three heads – reflected her comfort in her current role: successful, well-compensated, and relatively pressure-free. What she didn't realize was that I saw in her the perfect embodiment of what our company needed: someone who could unite our technical and sales cultures. What I kept to myself was that we were in early discussions with TELUS about acquiring the company.

Her success in the VP of Sales role exceeded even my optimistic expectations. She quickly established herself as a trusted broker between sales and technical teams, earning respect from both sides through her ability to understand and articulate their perspectives.

After the TELUS acquisition, our paths diverged professionally but we remained connected. Our relationship evolved into one of trusted confidants, with Tanya often seeking my counsel on professional challenges. As life circumstances changed (her divorce and my single status), our friendship gradually transformed into something deeper.

The transition from professional friendship to romantic relationship was approached cautiously at first. We kept our relationship private initially, concerned about workplace perceptions. What we discovered, however, was that we had each independently developed clear visions of what we wanted in a future partner, including personality traits, compatibility factors, and temperament. As our relationship deepened, we found ourselves checking off these predetermined criteria one by one.

In my opinion, our story validates my belief that the strongest romantic relationships often grow from foundations of friendship. The shared understanding, respect, and trust we developed as colleagues provided a solid base for our romantic relationship. Now, after more than two decades together, I can say with certainty that what began as professional admiration has evolved into one of the most fulfilling relationships of my life.

The experience taught me valuable lessons about both professional and personal relationships: the importance of recognizing potential in others, the value of building connections based on genuine respect and understanding, and the truth that sometimes the best partnerships grow naturally from shared experiences and mutual appreciation. Most importantly, it's shown me that life often has unexpected plans for us and being open to new possibilities while honoring our past can lead to profound happiness.

Limits to Growth: Hitting a Glass Ceiling

Even though I was thriving at TELUS – successfully leading division turnarounds and gaining valuable experience – I had hit an invisible ceiling. I managed several important divisions and delivered consistent results, yet promotion to the next executive level remained frustratingly out of reach. The gap between my current compensation and the next tier was significant, and no level of performance seemed enough to bridge it. It was time to face reality: I had reached the limits of my growth potential within TELUS. I knew it was time for (another) change. In a candid conversation with Joe Natale, my supervisor and presumed successor to Entwistle, I suggested it was time for me to leave TELUS. His gracious response and support in negotiating a fair severance package exemplified professional leadership, providing me the freedom to explore new opportunities.

Experience had taught me that finding the right executive position is a full-time job. It wouldn't be fair to TELUS – or effective for my search – to try balancing my current responsibilities with an active job hunt. The severance package would provide both the time and financial freedom to conduct a proper search. After multiple successful career transitions, I had developed the confidence to know I was highly employable and the faith to believe an even greater opportunity awaited. While I would miss many aspects of TELUS, particularly the corporate band, I knew this was the right decision for my career progression.

The Power of Network: Your All-Star Team Steps Up Again

Once again, I found myself at a career crossroads, but this time with a crucial advantage: a well-developed network built over decades of professional relationships. My experiences leaving LePage and navigating through the dot-com era had taught me the importance of maintaining and nurturing professional relationships even when you don't immediately need them. Given that I had now moved through five different companies in three different industries, my network expanded exponentially. Like a veteran player who's built relationships with coaches and scouts across multiple teams, my diverse career path had created a deep bench of professional connections I could call upon.

This situation perfectly illustrated the Network component of our GRAND SLAM framework in action. Just as a baseball team relies on its farm system and scouting network to identify new talent, I could now lean on the professional relationships I'd cultivated throughout my career.

The value of a strong network becomes most apparent during career transitions. What made my network truly powerful was its depth and authenticity. These weren't just casual acquaintances – they were people with whom I'd shared experiences, challenges, and successes. When I reached out during this transition, they didn't simply forward job postings. Instead, they became active advocates, opening doors and making personal recommendations. Former colleagues, business associates, and even past competitors stepped up to help, demonstrating the real value of maintaining professional relationships.

One of my mentors once shared a perspective that proved prophetic: "Your network is like a garden – it needs constant tending, but when you need it to bear fruit, it will provide more than you can harvest." As opportunities began flowing in from relationships I'd cultivated years earlier, I witnessed the truth of these words firsthand. Connections I'd made in one context were now creating opportunities I couldn't have imagined when first establishing them.

The Power of Connected Networks: When Opportunity Meets Preparation

Life has a fascinating way of bringing opportunities through unexpected channels, often demonstrating how our various networks can intersect in surprising and beneficial ways. I also think that there is an element of luck. Such was the case shortly after my departure from TELUS, when a sequence of events perfectly illustrated the power of maintaining relationships and the importance of having people in your network who truly understand your capabilities and aspirations.

Peter Cullen and I had known each other through our membership in TEC (The Executive Committee), a peer group for CEOs and senior executives. While we had developed a collegial relationship through our TEC meetings, sharing insights and experiences around the table with other executives, our connection hadn't extended much beyond those sessions. Like many professional relationships, ours was cordial but not particularly close.

What I didn't know at the time was that Peter was quietly exploring the acquisition of a struggling company, conducting his due diligence with characteristic discretion. Similarly, Peter was unaware that I was in the market for a new opportunity following my departure from TELUS. We were like two puzzle pieces that could fit together perfectly, but neither of us knew the other piece was available.

Enter Basile Papaevangelou, a mutual friend and consummate connector. Basile possessed what Malcolm Gladwell would call a "connector's gift," the ability to see potential synergies between people and opportunities. He knew of Peter's interest in acquiring the company and understood the type of leadership it would require to turn it around. He was also aware of my situation and, more importantly, recognized how my experience in managing organizational transformations could be exactly what Peter's potential acquisition needed. It was like having an all-star scout who could spot talent that others missed, someone who understood both what the team needed and what the player could bring to the game.

This situation perfectly illustrates a key principle about professional networks: sometimes the most valuable connections come through indirect links, through people who understand both parties well enough to see potential matches that the principals themselves might miss. Basile's role as a connector went beyond simple introduction – he understood the context, timing, and potential fit at a deeper level than either Peter or I could have at that moment. Sometimes the best trades in baseball aren't about finding someone who's already playing your position but recognizing talent that can be developed in a new role. My transition to Nutech Engineering proved to be exactly that kind of opportunity.

Robotics – what me?

Shortly thereafter, Peter brought me into Nutech Engineering as President to help accelerate the business. Nutech's business was to integrate industrial robots and associated technology to provide tier 2 auto parts manufacturing companies and tier 1 aerospace parts manufacturing companies with robotic capability to produce parts for automobiles and aircraft. What did I know about this business? Not much, but it was very similar to Arqana at a very high level. Emboldened by my experience at Arqana and TELUS, I felt incredibly confident that the challenge wasn't about the core business; it was inevitably around people performance.

NuTech had approximately 50 employees. Approximately 15 of the staff were Professional Engineers who developed the specification for the equipment the company would produce including the required automation (robotics), the custom equipment to integrate the robotics into the final solution, and the programming of the computers controlling the systems. Approximately 30 of the staff were manual laborers – people who build the systems the engineers would design. These included those who operated material fabrication machines and general shop floor workers. The balance of the staff were sales, finance, and administration. There were a lot of moving parts to the operation (pun intended).

Policies and Procedures:
The Cornerstone of Organizational Excellence

"Quality is not an act; it is a habit." – Aristotle

But before we continue with this story, I want to highlight something specific about me. For as long as I can remember I have been a big fan of policies and procedures. Perhaps it was my early training in music, where things follow a pre-set pattern, or simply something that was innate. It's always been something that has been important to me. Just as a championship baseball team relies on consistent practice routines, businesses thrive on well-established policies and procedures.

I remember reading the book The E-Myth Revisited by Michael E. Gerber. It is a wonderful parable where Gerber advocates for the development of systematic processes and procedures that enable a business to function independently of the leader's direct involvement. Gerber challenges the reader to think of their business as if they are going to franchise it. As such, you will need precise instructions on most aspects of the business. These policies and procedures not only facilitate a more organized workflow but also allows for the empowerment of employees, who can execute their roles with clarity and accountability. His profound question is "are you working in the business or are you working on the business," the primary difference being that if you're working in the business, you're not working to make the business systemic and better.

By focusing on designing a business as a franchise prototype – complete with documented systems – an environment is created where consistent quality and customer satisfaction thrive. Research from the Harvard Business Review supports this approach, showing that companies with well-documented processes are 31% more likely to achieve their strategic goals.

The Ultimate Process Framework: ISO Love This

One of the major redeeming qualities of Nutech Engineering was that they had already gone through the process of becoming an ISO 9001 certified company. An ISO 9001 certified company adheres to a globally recognized standard for quality management systems (QMS), demonstrating its commitment to consistently meeting customer and regulatory requirements while enhancing customer satisfaction. This certification signifies that the organization has implemented a robust framework of processes and procedures that focus on quality assurance, continuous improvement, and risk management.

Although I did not have any previous experience with ISO or any other standards organization, this was a mecca for a policy and procedure geek like me.

The promise of an ISO 9001 certified company is to ensure that its products and services not only meet established quality benchmarks but also align with the strategic objectives of the business. This certification not only fosters a culture of excellence within the organization but also enhances its credibility and competitiveness in the marketplace, making it a trusted partner for clients and stakeholders. In many fields, customers demand this certification.

Research by the International Organization for Standardization shows that ISO 9001 certified companies demonstrate:

- 57% higher customer satisfaction rates.

- 48% reduction in operational inefficiencies.

- 34% increase in market competitiveness.

While I was no stranger to policies and procedures, I was certainly not aware of the discipline at this level. Moreover, this was such an important element that they had the head of quality reporting directly to me as the president. Talk about making a powerful statement.

I quickly embraced all of what the discipline involved including documented procedures. In order to retain your certification, an organization needs to undergo an external audit on a regular basis. What I quickly learned is that any major infractions of the ISO Standard could put your certification at risk. But I also came to understand that most of the time if people were not compliant in an audit it was not because they were not following some ISO Standard. It was because they were not following the policies and procedures that they themselves created.

Picture this, a company goes to the time and expense of defining and documenting detailed processes by which they are going to govern virtually all aspects of their business. This is all submitted with a broader application for ISO certification. The international organization then certifies the company subject to periodic audits. The company then goes on not to follow the policies and procedures that they put in place. What? Well, that is what I came to realize was not just a problem with Nutech Engineering; it was a problem with many companies.

The remedy for this was surveillance audits. These were mock audits typically performed by employees in their spare time. Another process and procedure; how could I not love it?

What we would do is get people from outside of one function to review current projects from outside of their area of responsibility. Specifically, engineers would review the work from people on the shop floor, people on the shop floor would review sales and marketing processes, and procedures and sales marketing and finance would review engineering procedures. This forced individuals to explain things in very simple terms. It also had the redeeming quality of promoting education for individuals in areas outside of their day-to-day responsibilities.

This approach, similar to what Google calls "reverse mentoring," broke down silos and fostered organizational learning. Studies by Deloitte show that companies with strong cross-functional collaboration are twice as likely to outperform their peers.

I remember very distinctly one of the most junior people in our organization interviewing me. As you might expect, he was a bit nervous and anxious about grilling the president. But I knew what was at stake and so I kept encouraging him to be brutal with his questions. Similarly, I encouraged everyone at our all-hands meetings to be tough on each other. The results were very impressive. Not only did we pass our external audit with flying colors, our auditor also was very complimentary on several of the processes that we had implemented.

What I took away from this experience was that success isn't about perfection but consistent improvement. Whether through ISO certification or less formal systems, the key is creating a culture of disciplined execution. McKinsey research indicates that organizations with strong process management cultures show 30% higher levels of employee engagement and 25% better financial performance.

You do not necessarily need to go to the extent of ISO certification to achieve many of the benefits. Simply adhering to the rigor and discipline will yield most of the results.

Here is how I think policies and procedure exemplifies the Consistency Effect:

- Systematic approach to quality through regular, repeatable processes

- Continuous improvement through regular audits and feedback

- Building organizational muscle memory through consistent practice

- Creating sustainable success through documented procedures

- Developing a culture of excellence through regular habits

Key Takeaways:

1. Process Documentation is Critical

- Well-documented procedures create scalable, sustainable operations.

- Clear processes enable consistent quality delivery.

- Documentation supports knowledge transfer and organizational learning.

2. Cross-Functional Understanding Drives Success

- Internal audits by different departments increase organizational knowledge.

- Breaking down silos improves overall operational effectiveness.

- Diverse perspectives enhance process improvement.

3. Culture of Continuous Improvement

- Regular audits maintain high standards.

- Employee involvement in process improvement increases engagement.

- Systematic approach to quality becomes self-reinforcing.

4. Leadership Commitment Matters

- Leaders must model process adherence.

- Executive support legitimizes quality initiatives.

- Consistent leadership focus drives organizational buy-in.

This systematic approach to business operations, while sometimes seen as rigid, actually creates the foundation for sustainable success and innovation – much like how mastering the fundamentals in sports or any endeavor enables more advanced play.

7th Inning Stretch

To Coach or be Coached – Is that the Question?

"Education is not the filling of a pail, but the lighting of a fire." — W.B. Yeats

---

Section 1: The Foundation of Coaching

Before diving deeper into transformational leadership, let's explore the interconnected dynamics of coaching, being coached and managing people.

Just as a great baseball coach can transform talented individuals into a championship team, effective coaching in business can be the difference between mediocrity and excellence. Coaching isn't about downloading information into someone's mind; it's about igniting their potential and helping them discover their own path to success.

Think about your earliest role models. For baseball players, it might have been the stars on their baseball cards. In business, we all have those larger-than-life figures who shaped our understanding of leadership and success. These weren't just successful people; they were beacons showing us what was possible.

When the Student is Ready the Teacher will Appear: The Essence of Being Coachable

But mentorship isn't about being a fan in the bleachers. It's not about sitting back and waiting for wisdom to rain down on you like a shower of popcorn. It's about actively seeking out those relationships, showing up to practice ready to learn, and being willing to adjust your swing based on the feedback you get. And the absolute most important thing is that it's about being coachable.

Expanding on Coachability

Being coachable means embracing a mindset of continuous growth and learning. It's about recognizing that no matter how much you know or how skilled you are, there's always room for improvement. This mindset involves several key attributes:

1. Openness to Feedback:

Being coachable means being receptive to feedback, whether it's positive or constructive. It's about listening without defensiveness and understanding that feedback is a tool for growth. It's like watching the post-game tape – sometimes it's not pretty, but it's always instructive.

2. Willingness to Change:

Coachability requires a willingness to make changes based on the guidance you receive. This might mean stepping out of your comfort zone or adopting new methods and perspectives.

3. Humility:

A coachable person understands that they don't have all the answers. Humility allows you to acknowledge your limitations and learn from others who have different experiences and insights. Babe Ruth struck out 1,330 times.

4. Proactive Learning:

Instead of passively waiting for knowledge to come to you, being coachable involves actively seeking out learning opportunities. Don't wait for your coach to call you into their office. This could also be through reading, attending workshops, or engaging in conversations with mentors.

5. Consistency:

Eating isn't a one and done deal, and neither is coaching. Applying the advice and strategies shared by your mentors consistently is crucial. It's not enough to try something once and abandon it if it doesn't yield immediate results. Consistency helps to truly integrate new habits and techniques into your practice. It's about showing up day after day, putting in the work, and gradually improving your game.

6. Reflective Practice:

Reflecting on your progress and the feedback you receive is a vital part of being coachable. This means regularly evaluating what's working, what's not, and why. Reflective practice helps you make informed adjustments and continuously improve.

The Benefits of Being Coachable

"There are three kinds of men. The ones that learn by reading. The few who learn by observation. The rest of them have to pee on the electric fence for themselves."
— Will Rogers

This highlights the idea that different people learn in different ways, with some needing to experience things firsthand, even if it involves painful mistakes.

Being coachable can accelerate your personal and professional growth in numerous ways:

1. Enhanced Skill Development:

By being open to new ideas and techniques, you can quickly enhance your skills and expertise.

2. Better Relationships:

Coachability fosters better relationships with mentors and colleagues as it demonstrates your commitment to growth and improvement.

3. Increased Opportunities:

Mentors are more likely to invest time and resources in someone who is coachable, leading to more opportunities for advancement and success.

4. Greater Resilience:

A coachable mindset helps build resilience as you learn to adapt and grow from challenges and setbacks.

From Player to Coach - The Evolution of Leadership

As my career progressed, I continued to seek out coaches, recognizing it as a crucial component of ongoing growth and success. The perspective gained from these experiences was invaluable, often providing the clarity needed to navigate complex business challenges.

My own journey in business has been profoundly shaped by coaching, both formal and informal. I've learned as much from observing the missteps of others as I have from witnessing exemplary leadership. This realization led me to an important conclusion: in a sense, everyone can be a coach. Every interaction, every observed success or failure, carries a lesson if we're attuned to it.

The transition from individual contributor to leader represents one of the most significant shifts in any professional journey. It's like moving from being a star player to becoming a coach – the skills that made you successful on the field aren't necessarily the same ones you'll need in the dugout.

But here's a crucial point: the best coach isn't necessarily the best player. In fact, some of the most successful coaches in both sports and business were never star performers themselves. What sets them apart is their ability to observe, analyze, and communicate, to see the game from a perspective that players, caught up in the moment-to-moment action, might miss.

Consider the business world. A CEO coach doesn't need to have built a billion-dollar company to offer valuable insights to an aspiring entrepreneur.

What they need is a keen understanding of business dynamics, human psychology, and the ability to identify and nurture potential. They're the ones who can spot a flaw in your swing before it costs you the game or identify a blind spot in your business strategy before it becomes a costly mistake.

The hardest lesson for many new leaders – myself included – is learning to step back and let others take the swing. When you've built your career on being the person who gets things done, it's tempting to jump in and "fix" situations yourself. But effective leadership means resisting this urge. Instead of being the hero who saves the day, your role becomes creating heroes, identifying potential in others, providing opportunities for growth, and offering the right balance of challenge and support. It's like a batting coach who knows when to offer technical advice and when to simply provide encouragement.

Perhaps the most profound aspect of this transition is the shift in how you derive satisfaction from your work. As an individual contributor, success is immediate and personal – you can see the direct results of your efforts. In leadership, success becomes more nuanced and long-term. Your greatest achievements might be watching team members develop capabilities they didn't know they had, seeing them tackle challenges they once thought impossible, or building a culture of collaboration and excellence that sustains itself even in your absence.

The most effective leaders, I've found, never completely lose their "player" mindset. They maintain their understanding of the front-line challenges and their passion for the game. But they combine this with a coach's perspective: the ability to see the bigger picture, to develop strategies that leverage diverse talents, and to build teams that are greater than the sum of their parts. This dual perspective (understanding both the player's challenges and the coach's responsibilities) becomes a powerful tool for building high-performing teams and developing future leaders.

The ultimate measure of leadership success isn't in your personal statistics anymore; it's in the growth and achievements of your team, the strength of the culture you build, and the legacy you leave through the leaders you develop. Just as a great coach's influence extends far beyond their immediate team through the players they've mentored, effective business leadership creates ripple effects that continue long after you've moved on to new challenges.

The Power of Questions: What does Greek philosophy have to do with Business?

As a coach, you're standing on a mound of knowledge, facing someone who's struggling with a challenge. You could shout instructions from your perch, telling them exactly what to do and how to do it. But in the past, how many times have you told someone something only to watch it sail right past them like a missed fastball?

Why do you think that was? Did they understand the information? Did they need to agree with it? Did they need to decide that they wanted to do something about it? Or some combination of all three? Doesn't that seem like a lot of bases to cover – consciously or subconsciously?

What if you perfected a powerful coaching technique that's been around for thousands of years? Would you believe me if I said it would positively change the foregoing outcome dramatically? It's like discovering a secret pitch that baffles every batter!

If you asked someone questions that led them to come to their own conclusions, how might that change their response to your advice? What if by asking great questions instead of giving answers, you could help people clear their own hurdles of understanding, agreement, and motivation to act? How might that change your approach to coaching? It's like turning every coaching session into a little league game where everyone wins!

When someone figures something out for themselves, they truly get it. It's not just information; it's insight and it becomes their insight. If it's their idea, they're already on board. No need to convince them. People are more likely to act on their own conclusions than someone else's instructions. That is the underrated power of questions.

Consider this: when someone arrives at an answer through their own thinking, do they need to be convinced that they understand it? agree with it? Or that it is the right solution for them? Or have they already decided all of those things for themselves?

Think about a time when you figured something out for yourself. How did that feel compared to being told the answer? Did you feel more invested in the solution?

Socrates, that all-star philosopher of ancient Greece, figured out this winning strategy centuries ago. He realized that when you ask someone a question, you're not just making conversation – you're inviting them to step up to the plate of their own understanding.

In the foregoing paragraphs, I have tried to demonstrate the Socratic method, which is arguably less effective in written form than it is in dialogue. A little like the difference between watching a baseball game on TV and actually stepping up to the plate yourself.

Some might ask the question "isn't this manipulation?" Great question. Isn't telling someone what to do a formal manipulation? At the end of the day, if you ask great questions and someone concludes, they feel comfortable with, is this manipulation or is it helping them? I believe it's the latter.

Here is the absolute double-header bonus, even if the person you are asking questions to fully understands what you are doing, and assuming your questions are thought-provoking and respectful, they never see the situation as being unpleasant. In my experience, it's quite the opposite. Aren't questions a way of changing the dynamic of a conversation because you're not telling somebody what to do or think, you're asking their thoughts on something? Isn't it a more respectful and powerful way of communicating in general?

But what about the time involved? Does it take more time upfront to pitch empowering and thought-provoking questions than it does to repeatedly tell someone something that they never really seem to do? Are the results worth it? When someone comes to the conclusion you want them to reach, what questions could you ask to reinforce their conclusion? When they reach a conclusion, you do not think is correct, what questions could you ask to guide their thinking in a different direction? It's like spending extra time in batting practice to perfect your swing – it might take longer, but the results speak for themselves.

In the end, is the Socratic method just about asking questions or is it an eloquent and empowering way for others to find their answers and turn every interaction into a potential breakthrough of understanding? By reflecting on all these questions, what was your experience with the Socratic method? How did it feel to ponder your own answers to the questions?

Isn't the job of a great coach to develop the mental agility in others to solve problems independently? They're not just handing out signals from the sidelines – they're teaching others to read the field and make smart plays on their own. It's about turning every player into a potential MVP.

The Power of Belief: The Coach's Secret Weapon

"Believe in people more than they believe in themselves, until they believe in themselves as much as you do." Les Brown, author, Live your Dreams

The notion of believing in others more than they believe in themselves isn't just a modern Silicon Valley mantra; it's a leadership philosophy with deep roots. Harvard psychologist Robert Rosenthal proved it with a study that was basically a Jedi mind trick in a lab coat. He told teachers that certain randomly selected students had potential for "unusual intellectual gains." Lo and behold, those students' IQs rose faster than their peers'. It's like the teachers' beliefs were a cognitive growth hormone!

This phenomenon taps into a fundamental human truth: many of us are carrying around a hefty amount of self-doubt. Many of us are afraid of taking risks, being wrong, or, heaven forbid, being ourselves.

Unleashing Potential: The Art of Building Confidence in Others

"It's not that people don't know what to do, it's that they don't do what they know." Bob Proctor, author, You Were Born Rich

As a leader, your most powerful role is that of a catalyst: someone who helps others recognize and achieve their full potential. This isn't just about offering generic encouragement; it's about providing specific, meaningful recognition and celebrating achievements of all sizes.

As referenced earlier, my experience at TELUS provided numerous insights into this leadership approach. I discovered that most performance issues weren't about capability – people generally knew what to do. Rather, it was about confidence –

they were hesitant to act on their knowledge, often paralyzed by fear of failure or career consequences. Having accumulated years of experience and achieved a certain level of financial security, I found myself in a position to take risks that others might shy away from.

This realization led me to develop a simple but powerful leadership strategy: I would tell my team members that if our initiatives succeeded, they would receive all the credit, but if they failed, I would shoulder the blame. At first, this approach bewildered many team members. In a corporate culture often characterized by self-preservation and individual achievement, such an offer seemed almost suspicious. Why would anyone willingly take the blame while giving away the credit?

The answer was simple: I believed that true leadership success comes from team achievement, not personal accolades. By removing the fear of failure and providing a safety net, I could help talented people take the risks necessary for innovation and growth. This approach did more than protect team members – it empowered them to stretch beyond their comfort zones and discover capabilities they didn't know they possessed.

The results of this leadership approach exceeded even my most optimistic expectations. Each successful initiative acted like a stepping stone, building team members' confidence and encouraging them to take on increasingly ambitious challenges. Success bred success in a powerful upward spiral. As people saw their ideas work and received recognition for their achievements, they became more willing to propose and implement innovative solutions.

What proved particularly fascinating was the contagious nature of this success. Other team members, observing their colleagues' achievements and the positive recognition they received, began to shed their own risk aversion. The "safety net" approach created a culture in which innovation wasn't just permitted – it was expected and celebrated. Instead of sticking to safe, conventional methods, team members actively sought opportunities to improve processes and challenge the status quo.

We moved from a group that followed established procedures to one that constantly questioned and improved them. The results were measurable: higher performance metrics, improved efficiency, and perhaps most importantly, increased job satisfaction and engagement. This experience reinforced a crucial leadership lesson: when you remove the fear of failure and replace it with the confidence to innovate, people will consistently exceed your expectations. They just need someone to believe in them first.

Think of confidence like a plant needing water to grow. As a leader, your belief in others provides that essential nourishment. Too little support leaves potential withering on the vine; too much can overwhelm and create dependency. The art lies in finding the right balance: providing enough encouragement to foster growth while allowing space for independent development.

When you master this balance, you become more than a manager. You become a transformer of talent, helping people convert their self-doubt into self-assurance and their hesitation into action. The results often exceed expectations, as people freed from the fear of failure often achieve things they never thought possible.

The Leadership Paradox

In leadership, I often find that I am trying to bridge disparate concepts, both of which may have considerable merit. Here are two seemingly contradictory yet complementary approaches to people that have been a driving force in my leadership and coaching style.

The Rockefeller Principle:

John D. Rockefeller believed great leaders could inspire ordinary people to achieve extraordinary results. His approach focused on creating an environment where potential could flourish, providing the vision, support, and motivation needed for people to exceed their own expectations. This has always been a mantra I have tried to live by. In fact, many times when I look at a situation in which an employee is not performing, I will always first look at who is managing them.

The Rohn Method:

Jim Rohn, one of Tony Robbins' mentors, advocated for "being in the behavior attraction business, not the behavior management business." His philosophy centered on hiring people who have the skills, talent, and attitude you want to have on your team rather than trying to change people. I also subscribe to this view.

Synthesizing Success:

The perspectives of Rockefeller and Rohn, on the surface appear to be polar opposites. However,

I have come to see that the two views can be harmonized if seen as complementary guideposts rather than absolute rules. When performance issues arise, your first instinct shouldn't be replacement but inspiration and development. However, when change is necessary, focus on recruiting individuals whose behaviors and attitudes will enhance your team's capabilities.

Mastering Delegation - The Art of Letting Go Without Dropping the Ball

In the complex game of leadership, delegation stands as one of the most crucial skills to master. Like a perfectly executed pitch in baseball, when delegation is done well, it can lead to spectacular results. However, when mishandled, it can cost you the game.

Andrew Carnegie, one of history's most successful industrialists, understood this principle intimately when he stated that "delegation is not abrogation." So how do you strategically distribute the workload to leverage your team's strengths while keeping your eye on the ball?

The challenges of delegation are perhaps best illustrated by the famous parable about responsibility: "This is a story about four people named Everybody, Somebody, Anybody, and Nobody. There was an important job to be done. Everybody was sure that Somebody would do it. Anybody could have done it, but Nobody did it..." Confused? That's exactly the point. When delegation and responsibility isn't clear, you can end up with a mess. It is like two outfielders who fail to communicate over a fly ball and run into each other and allow the other team to get a double or home run.

Effective delegation begins with clear communication. Leaders must articulate their expectations with precision, defining specific objectives and desired outcomes that leave no room for misinterpretation. The Balanced Scorecard is a perfect tool to assist with this task.

Resource support forms the second cornerstone of successful delegation. Just as a baseball team needs proper equipment and training facilities to succeed, your team members need the right tools, training, and access to information to perform their tasks effectively. Creating an environment for success goes beyond just providing resources – it involves fostering team capability and confidence through ongoing support and development.

Progress monitoring requires the delicate touch of a skilled coach watching from the dugout. Louis V. Gerstner Jr., the guy who turned around IBM, once said, "People don't do what you expect but what you inspect." But the key lies in maintaining awareness without micromanaging, much like a coach who observes his players but lets them play their game. Regular check-ins, open communication lines, and early intervention when challenges arise ensure that delegated tasks stay on track without stifling initiative or creativity.

One of my mentors, Rowland Fleming, offered a profound insight into the persistent communication required for effective delegation: "When you are sick of the words coming out of your mouth – the last person in your organization is just starting to get it." This wisdom aligns perfectly with the "Rule of Seven" in marketing, the principle that people need to hear something seven times before it truly registers. This reminds us that effective delegation requires patience, persistence, and consistent reinforcement of expectations (aka communications).

This accountability framework represents perhaps the most nuanced aspect of delegation. While the leader remains ultimately accountable for outcomes, successful delegation requires empowering team members and building trust through partnership. This process creates opportunities for learning from both successes and failures, ultimately developing future leaders within the organization.

Finding and Leveraging Mentorship

In addition to the coaching one receives through superiors, there are many other ways to enhance your learning journey. However, finding the right mentor isn't about waiting for someone to discover you – it's about taking intentional action. Throughout my career, I have been fortunate that many of my most impactful mentors appeared magically throughout my journey. However, I could have received much more valuable mentoring had I pursued these and other relationships through deliberate engagement and clear communication.

Taking the Initiative

Many potential mentors hesitate to offer guidance uninvited, concerned about overstepping boundaries. I've learned this firsthand when senior executives later told me they would have offered more guidance if I had explicitly asked. This taught me an important lesson: don't wait for mentorship to find you; be direct in seeking it out.

It is important to consider multiple paths to finding mentors. Your existing network, including family and friends, might connect you with potential mentors. Industry boards and professional organizations often provide natural environments where mentoring relationships develop organically. Community leadership initiatives frequently lead to connections with senior executives who can provide valuable guidance. Even within your current organization, leaders whose career paths inspire you might become valuable mentors. The key is to ask.

I think you will be surprised how many leaders will jump at the chance to mentor an up-and-coming leader. If there is someone in your network/life that you feel you could learn from through a mentoring relationship, it's worth taking the initiative to ask whether they would be interested.

How to Approach Mentorship

Approach potential mentors with clear objectives for what you hope to learn, specific examples of why you value their experience, and realistic expectations about time commitment. Most importantly, consider how you can add value in return. The best mentoring relationships are two-way streets.

One of the most valuable lessons in my leadership journey came from realizing that mentorship isn't always top-down.

When I joined TELUS, I faced a challenge that may be familiar to anyone who transitions into a new industry. While my leadership skills were solid, my technical knowledge in the telecommunication field was lacking and the industry jargon felt like a foreign language. The traditional solution of seeking guidance from senior executive peers proved impractical. While my peers were willing to help me, their packed schedules meant constantly cancelled meetings and fragmented learning.

Then I had what I thought was a novel idea. I approached a senior leader in TELUS' technical group with a specific request. "Do you have a promising individual on your team who is technically brilliant but would benefit from some leadership/career coaching?" Much to my delight, he introduced me to Vlad Hashinski, a Technical Director. I approached Vlad with a proposition. "You coach me on all of the technical aspects that a senior leader should know, and I will give you leadership and career coaching in exchange." At first, he was a bit puzzled. This was not normal in TELUS at the time. However, after some encouragement, I was delighted that he took me up on my offer.

The real benefit of this sometimes-called reversed mentorship relationship was that we both treated the sessions with a very high level of importance. Rarely if ever did I reschedule. To the best of my recollection, Vlad never did. Both of us came to the meetings prepared with relevant agendas and supporting material. I offered strategic thinking frameworks, decision-making processes, and career navigation insights, while Vlad provided crucial knowledge about telephony technology and emerging trends. It was a truly mutually beneficial experience.

I believe that this approach is also valuable for senior level executives who are increasingly expected to keep up on the latest technological changes affecting their industry.

Making Mentorship Work

The best mentoring relationships, traditional or reverse, are built on mutual value exchange. Come prepared to each interaction with specific questions and follow through on advice received. Tell your mentor if you have followed their advice – everyone wants to know they made a difference. Provide regular updates on your progress, respect your mentor's time and commitments, and continuously look for opportunities to add value to your mentor's objectives.

Don't limit yourself to one mentor or one type of mentoring relationship. Different mentors can help with different aspects of your development, from industry expertise and leadership skills to technical knowledge and career navigation. Some mentors might guide you in specific areas like digital strategy or financial acumen, while others might help with broader career and life decisions.

As I learned early in my career, it is important to maintain a network and life outside work. I think that same guidance would apply to mentorships. Many corporations have mentorship programs which are designed to foster leadership and career progression within that specific organization. These arrangements are not always prioritized or taken as seriously as they should, and the benefits are not always there. Having mentors outside your current organization can often provide guidance that transcends your current role.

It's Never too Late to be a Mentor

Mentoring isn't about waiting around to be asked. I am certainly guilty of this. There are many times in my career when I saw others who could have benefitted from a mentoring relationship, and I didn't take the first step for fear of overstepping. I admit that this was a limiting belief on my part. I now have the belief that many people would like a mentor but are afraid to ask. I now take the first step, and it has been very rewarding.

What I have found is that the most effective mentoring relationships grow from genuine connection and mutual respect. Whether you're learning from a seasoned executive or an emerging technical expert, approach the relationship with authenticity, commitment, and a willingness to both learn and contribute. In today's rapidly evolving business environment, the ability to learn from everyone – regardless of age or position – has become a crucial leadership skill.

If you are interested in exploring mentorship further, please visit www.consistency-edge.com/pages/shop to review my document on Finding and Leveraging Mentorship: A Practical Framework.

The Art of Decision-Making: Momentum Over Perfection

"The journey of a thousand miles begins with one step."
— Confucius

One of the most pervasive and damaging pitfalls of leadership I've observed is the paralysis of indecision. Too often, capable leaders find themselves trapped in a web of procrastination or analysis paralysis, favoring inaction over the perceived risk of making a "wrong" choice. This fear-driven approach, while understandable, can be incredibly detrimental to both personal growth and organizational success.

Throughout my career, I've made thousands of decisions, each carrying its own weight of uncertainty and potential consequences. Yet, one crucial lesson I've learned is this: none of the decisions I have made in business have been life-or-death scenarios. Meaning, I never saw a decision as one so monumental that I or the business could not course correct if later we saw that a different decision needed to be made. Instead, decisions are like stepping stones, each one an opportunity to learn, adapt, and grow.

The key to effective decision-making lies not in achieving perfection, but in embracing the power of momentum. Every choice we make is based on the best information available at that moment. As situations unfold and new data emerges, we have the ability – and indeed, the responsibility – to make course corrections. This dynamic approach to leadership allows for flexibility and continuous improvement, qualities that are essential in our rapidly changing business landscape.

This situation reminds me of the lyrics to a song written by my favorite drummer Neil Pert of the Canadian rock band Rush, who was also the band lyricist. In their song "Freewill," the lyrics state, "If you choose not to decide, you still have made a choice." This line encapsulates a fundamental truth about decision-making: inaction is a decision, often with far-reaching consequences.

The beauty of embracing decisive action lies in its ability to generate momentum. It's this forward motion that truly drives progress and innovation. In fact, one could argue that the primary purpose of setting goals isn't necessarily to achieve them in their exact, predefined form, but rather to set individuals and organizations in motion. As Confucius said, "Roads were made for journeys, not destinations." This movement creates a positive feedback loop: as we progress, we gain new insights and information, allowing us to make more informed decisions and adjustments along the way.

This approach stands in stark contrast to the stagnation that results from indecision. When we refuse to make choices, we rob ourselves and our organizations of valuable learning opportunities. We miss out on the chance to test our theories, challenge our assumptions, and grow from both our successes and our failures. Recall our discussion about my time at TELUS where I removed the fear of failure to liberate the team to make decisions and move forward.

So, how can we cultivate this decisive mindset? Here are a few strategies:

1. Embrace imperfection: Recognize that there's no such thing as a perfect decision. Every choice carries both risks and opportunities.

2. Set clear priorities: Understand what truly matters in each situation. This clarity can help cut through the noise of overthinking.

3. Create a decision-making framework: Develop a systematic approach to evaluating options, which can help reduce the emotional burden of choice.

4. Practice "satisficing": Aim for decisions that are good enough to meet your criteria, rather than endlessly seeking the absolute best option.

5. Learn from every outcome: Whether a decision leads to success or setback, there's always

a lesson to be gleaned. Make reflection and adaptation part of your process.

6. Cultivate a culture of decisiveness: Encourage your team to make decisions at their level, fostering an environment of empowerment and accountability.

Remember, the goal isn't to make perfect decisions, but to make decisions perfectly – with confidence, purpose, and a willingness to adapt. By embracing this mindset, we free ourselves.

Just as in baseball, where a batter must decide in a split second whether to swing, hold, or adjust their position, business leaders must be prepared to make quick, informed decisions. We can't always wait for the perfect pitch – sometimes we need to be ready to hit a curveball out of the park. And even if we don't knock it out of the park every time, remember that consistent singles and doubles often win more games than occasional home runs.

Busy working vs busy work: Solve for the monkey.

"The main thing is to keep the main thing the main thing" - Stephen Covey, author, The 7 Habits of Highly Effective People

Decisions are generally undertaken to address or avoid a problem. In solving the problem, the areas we focus on and the activities we undertake are critical to our success.

In the book *Switch: How to Change Things When Change Is Hard*, author/brothers Dan and Chip Heath, use a metaphor to illustrate the concept of focusing on the core, often more challenging, aspects of a task rather than getting distracted by the easier, less critical components. In their metaphor, you are tasked with teaching a monkey to recite Shakespeare while standing on a pedestal.

Most folks would jump right in and start building that pedestal. It's easy, it's quick, and boy, does it feel good to see something tangible come together. But hold on a second – is that really the heart of the challenge here?

The real meat of this task, the part that's going to make or break your success, is getting that monkey to channel its inner Hamlet. That's where the real sweat, tears, and banana bribes come into play. It's the tough part, the part that'll have you pulling your hair out and questioning your life choices.

So why do we gravitate towards building pedestals when we should be working on our monkey's diction? Simple. It feels good to make visible progress, even if it's not the most crucial part of the task. It's tempting to focus on things besides the monkey. We often find ourselves busily tackling the easy stuff, the "low-hanging fruit," while the real, meaty problems sit there untouched.

To make electric vehicles feasible, building the car wasn't the problem; the monkey was developing batteries capable of powering a car for a few hundred miles. The lesson? Don't get distracted by the small, easy wins if they're not moving you towards your main goal.

So next time you're faced with a big challenge, ask yourself: Am I building pedestals, or am I teaching my monkey to speak? That's where real progress happens. Until you've solved the monkey, nothing else matters. Progress and momentum are awesome.

Fear, Uncertainty, and Doubt: The Self-Imposed Speed Bump

The term FUD (Fear, Uncertainty, and Doubt) originated in the technology industry, specifically attributed to IBM's marketing tactics in the 1970s. The term was first popularized by Gene Amdahl after he left IBM to start his own company. He claimed IBM salespeople were instructed to spread FUD about competitors' products to make customers question their reliability and compatibility. In business, it's often used as a competitive tactic in which a dominant player creates anxiety about switching to competitors' products or services.

While the concept of FUD originated in the technology industry, its most damaging manifestation often comes from within us. Through my years of coaching and leadership experience, I've observed how individuals frequently become their own worst enemies by nurturing internal narratives that create paralysis rather than progress.

The Power of Self-Generated FUD

While external FUD can be challenging, self-imposed FUD is particularly insidious because it operates like an internal saboteur, constantly undermining our confidence and capabilities. I've witnessed countless talented professionals who create elaborate stories about why they can't succeed, shouldn't take risks, or aren't ready for the next step in their careers. These self-limiting narratives become self-fulfilling prophecies, creating the very failures they fear.

The ancient parable about the two forces within us – Fear and Faith – perfectly illustrates this dynamic. One evening, an elder shared with their grandchild a story about a struggle that occurs within all people. The elder said, "My child, the struggle is between two forces within us. One is Fear. It carries anxiety, concern, uncertainty, hesitancy, indecision, and inaction. The other is Faith. It brings calm, conviction, confidence, enthusiasm, decisiveness, excitement, and action." The grandchild thought about it for a moment and then gently asked, "Which force prevails?" The elder replied, "The one you nurture."

In our professional lives, we are always choosing which narrative to nurture. When we feed our fears, we create a cycle of hesitation and missed opportunities. When we nurture faith in our abilities and potential, we create momentum toward success.

Transforming FUD into Courage

In my coaching practice, I've developed a straightforward approach to helping people recognize and transform their self-imposed FUD. The first step is awareness – helping individuals identify when they're creating their own obstacles through negative self-talk or unfounded assumptions. The next step is more challenging but crucial: consciously flipping the narrative 180 degrees.

The Courage-Certainty-Confidence Cycle

When we consciously choose to feed courage instead of fear, certainty instead of uncertainty, and confidence instead of doubt, we create a positive cycle that builds upon itself. Each small success reinforces our faith, making the next challenge easier to face. This isn't about ignoring legitimate risks or concerns; it's about approaching them from a position of strength rather than weakness.

Practical Implementation

To help individuals transform their FUD into positive energy, I encourage them to:

1. Identify their self-imposed limitations.
2. Challenge the validity of their fears.
3. Create alternative, empowering narratives.
4. Take small, consistent actions that build confidence.
5. Celebrate progress and learn from setbacks.

The Leadership Connection

As leaders, our ability to recognize and transform FUD, both in ourselves and our teams, becomes a crucial skill. When we model the courage to face uncertainty with confidence, we create an environment where others feel empowered to do the same. This was evident in the workspace transformations I led. By demonstrating confidence in the new approach rather than doubt, we helped others embrace change rather than fear it.

The Result

When we successfully transform FUD into its positive counterparts, we not only enhance our own performance but also create a ripple effect throughout our organizations. Teams become more innovative, individuals take more initiative, and the overall culture shifts from fear-based caution to confidence-based action.

Bottom of the 7th Inning Stretch

This segment explored the multifaceted nature of leadership, from being coachable to becoming an effective coach. Through examining various leadership approaches, from the Socratic method to the Rockefeller Principle and Rohn Method, we see how different styles can complement each other. The chapter demonstrates that effective leadership isn't about having all the answers, but about asking the right questions, building confidence in others, and mastering the art of delegation. Success in leadership comes not from personal achievement but from developing others and creating an environment where teams can excel.

Key Takeaways:

1. The Art of Coaching

- Being coachable is essential for leadership development.

- Great coaches aren't necessarily the best players.

- Questions are more powerful than direct instructions.

- Building confidence in others is a crucial leadership skill.

2. Leadership Philosophy

- Balance Rockefeller's inspiration with Rohn's behavior attraction.

- Remove fear of failure to encourage innovation.

- Believe in others more than they believe in themselves.

- Success comes from team achievement, not personal accolades.

3. Effective Delegation

- Clear communication is essential.

- Provide necessary resources and support.

- Monitor progress without micromanaging.

- Maintain ultimate accountability while empowering others.

4. Communication Excellence

- Messages need repeating multiple times.

- Questions are more effective than directives.

- Clear expectations drive better results.

- Regular reinforcement is crucial for success.

5. Team Development

- Focus on building others' confidence.

- Create safe environments for risk-taking.

- Celebrate team achievements.

- Develop future leaders through empowerment.

Bottom of the 7th Inning

Time for Another Change Up

Learning Objectives:

After reading this chapter, you will:

- Understand the importance of documented agreements in business relationships

- Learn effective job search strategies for senior executives.

- Master the art of strategic networking

- Understand how to leverage networks for career opportunities.

- Learn to craft effective networking approaches and follow-up strategies

- Recognize the value of maintaining networks during stable career periods

- Understand how reputation and past performance create future opportunities

"Verbal contracts aren't worth the paper they are written on." — Yogi Berra

From my earliest days in business, I was always taught that the best practice is to get everything in writing. Even if you're not able to have everything in a mutually agreed upon document, there are always ways to document conversations. One of the best ways is to follow up a verbal conversation with an email that summarizes the discussion, and any conclusions or agreements reached. Another way is to keep detailed notes which could be beneficial in a dispute or, worst case, a litigation.

In taking the role at NuTech Engineering, I had many conversations with Peter Cullen, whose style was very different from my own. We talked about turning around NuTech and then me taking on a further role with some of his other operating companies. He had a very strong dislike for contracts and legal forms. As we approached agreement on the terms of my engagement with NuTech, his aversion to a legal agreement became a major roadblock to the discussion. The coaching I received from our mutual friend Basile was that I should trust Peter at his word. Against my better judgement, I proceeded on good faith alone.

This turned out to be a colossal miscalculation on my part. Peter's analysis of NuTech's situation was that they were in a cash crunch situation with $2 million worth of receivables and approximately $2 million worth of payables. The task at hand was simple – collect receivables and pay the payables. Seemed straightforward enough. But once I took on the role and got into the chair as president, I quickly learned the receivables were tenuous at best, and there were more payables than were currently on the books. Consequently, the company continued to be in a cash crunch while Peter's other companies needed to fund the ongoing operation to prevent it from going into bankruptcy. This meant that cash was managed on a day-to-day basis. This was not something I had deep experience with. Nonetheless, it was a capability I soon mastered.

Although I helped the company manage these initial challenges, the prospects for the company were not as glowing as Peter had imagined. The 2007-2008 recession caused a sharp decline in auto sales as consumer confidence and credit availability plummeted. Major automakers like GM and Chrysler faced bankruptcy, leading to government bailouts to prevent collapse, while Ford managed to avoid bankruptcy through early loans. Supply chain disruptions and factory shutdowns worsened the financial strain on automakers and their suppliers. NuTech's business was highly dependent on the auto parts manufacturing industry which suffered along with the tier 1 automakers.

This was a situation I did not sign on for. Not only was it difficult to turn NuTech around, but Peter had selective amnesia about our broader discussion. Since there was nothing in writing, I needed to get to work on what was next.

Job Seeking as a Senior Leader

This time, I had no safety net; no severance package or other arrangements were negotiated with Peter. It was a painful lesson I never forgot.

Contrary to my situation when leaving TELUS, I had to set about finding a job while still fulfilling my obligations at NuTech. This time, the task was even harder given what was going on with the Global Financial Crisis.

While I was financially secure enough to cover my bills, the psychological pressure was intense. I felt like every day without a new position meant falling behind in my career trajectory. This anxiety drove me to approach my job search with an even higher level of intensity that I brought to my executive roles – manically developing strategic plans, setting goals and objectives, and working diligently from early morning onwards.

But this fear and anxiety haunted me constantly – 24 hours a day, seven days a week. The relentless pressure began affecting both my mental and physical health. I realized I needed to establish clear boundaries in my job search process. Just as with any executive role, I needed to create structure: dedicating specific hours for the search rather than letting it consume every moment. This wasn't just about finding my next position; it became a valuable lesson in developing perspective and practicing balance, skills that would serve me well in future leadership roles.

Initially, I sought to meet with senior level executive recruiters. I thought they would provide an easy path to the role I sought. I quickly realized that most executive recruiters work for companies, not people seeking jobs. If your skills and capabilities are not a fit for the assignment they have, they have little interest in you other than keeping your details in their files.

The statistic I received is that somewhere between 80 to 90% of jobs are from your network and only 10 to 20% from executive recruiters.

So, I set my sights on meeting with as many people as possible and I embraced every opportunity that came my way, embodying wisdom shared by a recruiter friend: "The networking gods favor those who put in the time."

Now, let's talk about networking, that essential business ritual that can feel like a cross between speed dating and a job interview. You've probably heard the famous adage attributed to John Wanamaker about advertising: "Half the money I spend on advertising is wasted; the trouble is I don't know which half." Well, I think the same principle applies to networking: 50% of your networking efforts might be wasted, but you never know which 50%.

It's like playing a game of "Networking Bingo," where half the squares lead to meaningful connections, and the other half are filled with small talk about the weather and politics. The key is to keep daubing those squares and shouting "Bingo!" at every opportunity (metaphorically, of course. We don't want security escorting you out of the networking event.)

The catch is you can't distinguish the wheat from the chaff until you are elbow-deep in dialogue. Similarly, you can't foresee which networking connection will be your golden ticket or just another addition to your contact list.

Here is another important lesson I learned. I would meet with people, and they would quickly ask, "So, what are you looking for?" My initial response was, "To find a leadership role in a medium sized company that is well run and profitable." I should not have been surprised to learn that most companies like that aren't looking for a new leader.

What I also learned is that the quality of your questions is the major determinant of the quality of the input you receive from the people you network with.

Effective networking for senior executive positions requires a focused, strategic approach that goes beyond general relationship building. The key is to concentrate your efforts on two specific groups: direct decision-makers who can hire you and well-connected individuals who can facilitate introductions to these decision-makers.

However, success lies not just in who you contact, but in how you frame your requests and manage these relationships. Specificity is crucial when engaging your network. Rather than making general requests for job leads, provide detailed information about your target industries, specific companies of interest, and the types of roles you're pursuing.

For example, instead of saying, "I'm looking for a senior executive position," you might say, "I'm interested in connecting with leaders in the technology integration space, particularly at companies like [specific examples] where my experience in scaling operations and managing transformational change could add value." This level of detail helps your contacts mentally scan their networks more effectively, often triggering connections that might not have occurred with a more general request.

The Art of the Soft Approach

One of the most effective networking strategies is to position your outreach as an information-gathering exercise rather than a direct job search. Instead of asking for job opportunities, request insights about an industry or company. This approach is less pressuring for both your contact and their network and often leads to more productive conversations. Many times, these informational meetings naturally evolve into discussions about opportunities, either within the contact's organization or through their network, simply because you've had the chance to demonstrate your expertise and value in a low-pressure setting.

Making It Easy for Your Network

Success in networking often comes down to reducing friction for those helping you. One of the most effective techniques I've found is to draft introduction emails for your contacts to use. Write these emails as if you were the referring party, making it easy for them to simply review, modify if needed, cut and paste into their email, and forward. Always structure these emails to remove your contact from any follow-up obligations by suggesting direct communication between you and the target contact. For example:

"Dear [Target Contact], I want to introduce you to [Your Name], who has an impressive track record in [relevant experience]. Given your expertise in [industry/company], I thought you might be willing to share your insights about [specific area of interest]. I'll leave it to you two to connect directly if you're willing to have that conversation.

Best regards, [Referring Contact's Name]"

The Follow-Up Factor

Perhaps the most crucial element of successful networking is consistent and appreciative follow-up. After each introduction or meeting, promptly inform your referring contact about the outcome. This accomplishes several important objectives: it demonstrates respect for their effort, keeps them engaged in your search, and makes them more likely to help again in the future.

A simple message like "Thank you again for introducing me to [name]. We had an excellent conversation about [topic], and I've gained valuable insights about [industry/company]. Your introduction was incredibly helpful."

This kind of follow-up builds your reputation as someone who values and respects others' time and efforts.

This systematic approach to networking – being specific about your targets, making it easy for others to help, and maintaining strong follow-up practices – transforms networking from a series of random connections into a strategic tool for senior executive career advancement.

The Cost of Neglected Networks

A common regret I hear from business colleagues is their failure to maintain active networking during stable periods of their careers. The pattern is sadly familiar: executives spend years, sometimes decades, with one organization, focusing entirely on internal relationships while letting their external networks atrophy. When unexpected changes occur, whether through downsizing, mergers, or other organizational shifts, they suddenly find themselves facing a daunting challenge. Without an active, current network, their job search becomes exponentially more difficult. It's like trying to build a baseball team from scratch in the middle of the season – possible, but far more challenging than maintaining one throughout the year.

This situation powerfully illustrates why networking shouldn't be viewed as a periodic activity tied to job searching, but rather as an essential, ongoing component of career management. The mountain these colleagues face when trying to rebuild neglected networks from scratch serves as a compelling reminder of why consistent networking throughout one's career is so crucial.

The Power of Consistency in Executive Networking

The principles of the Consistency Effect are particularly evident in executive networking, where success rarely comes from sporadic, intense bursts of activity. Whoever employs a sustained, methodical effort will flourish. Just as in baseball, where consistent base hits ultimately produce more runs than occasional one-off grand slam, effective networking requires regular, purposeful actions rather than intermittent, aggressive campaigns. This means maintaining a steady rhythm of outreach, follow-up, and relationship nurturing, even when immediate results aren't visible. Equally important is building and nurturing your work even when you're not looking for an opportunity.

I've found that dedicating time each week to networking activities (whether that's reaching out to new contacts, following up with existing ones, or sharing relevant insights and updates) creates a compound effect over time.

One of the methods I have used to keep in relevant contact with people in my network is to set a Google alert for their company. This way, each time they or their company was in the news I would get an alert. This gave me the opportunity to send a quick note and to congratulate, comment, or otherwise inquire about something that had recently happened. It's a small thing but it shows that you're interested.

Announcements are another excellent opportunity to keep track. Following them on LinkedIn, X, Facebook, or other social media gives you an opportunity to see what's going on in their life. They may have been appointed to a not-for-profit organization or received a promotion at work. These are excellent times to reach out and connect. Sometimes, these events remind you that you haven't spoken to them for a long time. This can create the opportunity to invite them for breakfast, lunch, or a coffee.

Also, when someone is between jobs, they are usually at their most vulnerable. This is an excellent time to reach out and support them in any way. Sometimes it's simply being available to brainstorm with them; other times it may be to help to connect them with people in your network. Either way, your contacts will remember you more fondly when you have supported them in their hour of need.

Finally, with other more important contacts, you can use a customer relationship management database to specify the frequency with which you want to follow up with them. It doesn't always have to be face-to-face. It can be simply a reminder to write them an email or give them a call. This consistency helps maintain momentum and keeps you top of mind within your professional network. Moreover, consistent networking builds credibility and trust; people are more likely to make meaningful introductions or share opportunities with someone they see as reliably engaged and professional rather than someone who only appears when they need something.

Another often underappreciated activity is engaging with people who are looking for help. These are people in the same boat as you, looking for opportunities and looking to work. I always make it a point of meeting with anyone who is looking for help as a form of paying it forward. I'm a big believer in karma. I also often coach people looking for a job with many of the same principles outlined above. Over the years, these people will remember you much more fondly than those that didn't have the time for them in their hour of need.

The same discipline that drives other aspects of the Consistency Effect – showing up daily, maintaining high standards, and focusing on incremental progress – applies equally to networking. Just as a batter doesn't expect every at-bat to result in a hit, not every networking interaction will lead directly to an opportunity. However, the cumulative effect of consistent, professional networking activity creates a powerful foundation of relationships and opportunities that can be activated when needed. This approach transforms networking from a reactive job-search tool into a proactive career management strategy that aligns perfectly with the Consistency Effect's emphasis on sustainable, long-term success through regular, disciplined action.

The Hidden Power of Networks: Unexpected Pathways to Opportunity

Networks often work in mysterious and fascinating ways, creating connections and opportunities through channels we might never directly observe. My journey to becoming Chief Operating Officer at Gibraltar Solutions perfectly illustrates this phenomenon. The opportunity didn't come through a direct network contact, but rather through a series of interconnected relationships that I hadn't even realized existed, like ripples in a pond reaching shores I couldn't see.

The story began when an executive recruiter conducted a search for a leadership role at Gibraltar. As part of their due diligence, they reached out to the client's customers and strategic partners, a smart practice that yielded unexpected results. Someone in one of these organizations was familiar with my work at Arqana Technologies, a company with a similar business model to their client.

This person, whose identity I never discovered, recommended me to the recruiter. It was a perfect example of how your reputation and work can create advocates you don't even know. While I couldn't trace the exact path of the referral, it was clear that the network I built through years of consistent performance and relationship building worked on my behalf even without my direct involvement.

When we think about networking, it's easy to focus on immediate, direct connections. However, my career experiences have repeatedly demonstrated that the true power of networking lies in its compound effect – the way relationships grow, intersect, and create unexpected opportunities over time. Just as compound interest builds wealth over time, compound networking builds opportunities through an ever-expanding web of connections and possibilities. Think of networking like a garden where you're constantly planting seeds. Some sprout quickly, others lie dormant for years, and still others cross-pollinate in ways you never expected. Every positive interaction, every project well executed, every relationship cultivated with integrity adds to your network's fertility.

The lesson for leaders is clear: approach every interaction with authenticity and a long-term perspective. Maintain relationships even when there's no immediate benefit, understanding that today's casual connection might become tomorrow's crucial link. In today's interconnected world, your reputation and relationships can create opportunities through channels you may never see or predict.

Bottom of the 7th Inning:

This part of the inning explores the critical importance of both documented agreements and strategic networking in career management. Through personal experiences with verbal agreements gone wrong and successful networking leading to unexpected opportunities, we see how the Consistency Effect applies to relationship building and career advancement. The chapter emphasizes that success in senior executive roles requires both proper documentation of agreements and the maintenance of strong professional networks. Most importantly, it demonstrates that networking isn't just about finding your next role; it's about building and maintaining relationships that create opportunities throughout your career.

Key Takeaways:

1. Documentation and Agreements

- Always get important agreements in writing.

- Document verbal conversations with follow-up emails.

- Trust should be verified through written agreements.

- Verbal contracts can lead to misunderstandings and disputes.

2. Strategic Job Search

- Job searching is a full-time commitment.

- Executive recruiters work for companies, not candidates.

- 80-90% of jobs come through networking.

- Specific, targeted networking is more effective than general outreach.

3. Effective Networking Approaches

- Focus on decision-makers and well-connected individuals.

- Be specific about target industries and roles.

- Use the "soft approach" of information gathering.

- Make it easy for contacts to help you.

- Maintain consistent follow-up practices.

4. Network Maintenance

- Build and maintain networks before you need them.

- Regular networking should be part of career management.

- Help others during their job searches.

- Consistent networking creates compound benefits over time.

5. The Consistency Effect in Networking

- Regular, sustained networking efforts outperform sporadic activity.

- Building relationships takes time and consistent effort.

- Every positive interaction can create future opportunities.

- Networks work in unexpected ways to create opportunities.

8th Inning

Learning from Experience:
The Power of Proper Documentation

"Experience is a hard teacher because she gives the test first, the lesson afterward." — Vernon Law

---

Learning Objectives:

After reading this chapter, you will:

- Understand how to navigate organizational change and transitions

- Learn to position yourself strategically within organizations

- Master the art of contract negotiations and protection

- Learn to manage complex client relationships

- Recognize the importance of institutional relationships

- Understand how leadership changes affect organizational dynamics

My transition to Gibraltar Solutions represented a crucial turning point in how I approached new opportunities, particularly regarding employment agreements. The painful lesson from NuTech, where verbal agreements proved as substantial as smoke, had left an indelible mark on my approach. While I was genuinely excited about the Gibraltar opportunity, my enthusiasm was tempered by hard-earned wisdom about the importance of proper documentation.

This time, I insisted on a thorough, well-documented process. Working closely with Gibraltar's owners, I focused on crafting comprehensive employment and shareholder agreements that would clearly define my role, responsibilities, and equity participation.

The employment agreement formed the foundation of our business relationship. At its core, this document needed to precisely outline my role description and reporting relationships within the organization. The compensation structure detailed not only the base salary but also established clear criteria for variable compensation and regular review periods. Performance expectations and evaluation metrics were clearly established to provide objective measures of success. The agreement also addressed crucial protective elements such as termination clauses, severance terms, and non-compete provisions. Intellectual property rights and confidentiality obligations were carefully defined, along with clear procedures for dispute resolution.

The shareholder agreement demanded equal precision, as it would govern the long-term relationship between all equity holders. We carefully outlined the share vesting schedule and conditions, ensuring alignment between commitment and ownership. The agreement established clear voting rights and decision-making authority, creating a framework for effective corporate governance. Board representation and structure were detailed to ensure proper oversight and strategic direction. We included comprehensive exit provisions, incorporating both tag-along and drag-along rights to protect all shareholders in case of a future sale. The agreement also established a clear methodology for share valuation in buy-sell scenarios, along with policies regarding dividends and capital calls. Rights of first refusal on share transfers were included to maintain control over ownership composition.

The stock option agreement required particular attention given its complexity and tax implications. We clearly specified the option grant size and strike price, establishing a fair framework for equity participation. The vesting schedule included carefully considered acceleration triggers for certain business scenarios. Exercise periods and conditions were clearly defined, along with a thorough explanation of tax implications and treatment. The agreement addressed various departure scenarios, ensuring fair treatment while protecting company interests. Anti-dilution provisions were included to protect option holders in future funding rounds, and change of control considerations were carefully outlined.

While this meticulousness extended the negotiation period, it was time well spent. Each detail we discussed and documented helped prevent potential future misunderstandings and established clear expectations for all parties. The thorough documentation process served as a roadmap for our business relationship, addressing not just current arrangements but potential future scenarios.

"Good fences make good neighbors" translates perfectly to business: good contracts make good business partnerships. These agreements provide clarity in times of success and protection in times of challenge, serving as both a foundation for growth and a framework for resolving potential disputes. The result was worth the extra effort: a clearly defined arrangement that gave me the confidence to fully commit to the opportunity.

This experience reinforced a crucial lesson: in business, enthusiasm for an opportunity should never override the necessity for proper documentation. Well-crafted agreements serve as both a foundation for success and a safety net for all parties involved, transforming abstract promises into concrete commitments that can withstand the test of time and changing circumstances.

Gibraltar Solutions: Building on Past Experience

Gibraltar Solutions operated in the early days of what would become cloud computing, specializing in computer virtualization, and secure remote access technologies. Their solutions allowed multiple virtual computers to run simultaneously on single physical machines, while also providing remote access capabilities through platforms like Citrix, VMware, and Microsoft Remote Desktop. This technology stack enabled seamless remote work experiences and efficient resource management across compute, storage, and networking resources. While Gibraltar served sophisticated corporate customers requiring specialized hardware, software, and integration services for complex computer systems, their revenue model remained heavily dependent on product sales rather than the more valuable recurring revenue streams from professional and managed services.

The business model was remarkably similar to Arqana's – a value-added reseller combining technology resale with professional services for enterprise clients.

This business model similarity meant I could apply many lessons learned from my Arqana experience, particularly the importance of building a stronger professional services component and developing recurring revenue streams to create more predictable, sustainable growth. The challenge would be implementing these changes while maintaining the company's existing strengths in product sales and technical expertise.

Leading by Example: The Power of Workspace Innovation

Leadership often requires challenging established norms, particularly when those norms conflict with an organization's potential for growth and innovation. My experiences across multiple organizations demonstrate how physical workspace decisions can powerfully signal leadership philosophy and drive cultural change. This insight didn't come to me immediately. It emerged from deliberately reflecting on past experiences and connecting seemingly unrelated dots across different roles and organizations. The power of retrospective analysis lies in taking time to pause, reflect, and ask yourself what past experiences might inform your current challenges. It's not enough to simply accumulate experiences; we must actively mine them for insights that can shape our present decisions and future directions.

At Gibraltar Solutions, my first leadership decision set the tone for broader organizational change. Upon arrival, I discovered the company had created an expansive office for me by combining two private offices - a traditional symbol of executive status. Instead of accepting this arrangement, I saw an opportunity to model what many technology companies were doing with workplace design. Drawing from my TELUS experience with flexible workspaces, I converted my designated office into a meeting room and initiated a broader transformation of our workspace culture. Despite initial resistance, we converted virtually all private offices into shared resources, naming them after customers and suppliers to reinforce our client-centric focus. This wasn't just about space efficiency; it was about creating a living demonstration of the remote access technology we were selling, with workstations showcasing different aspects of our solutions.

These workspace decisions reflect a broader leadership philosophy: actions speak louder than words. By willingly giving up traditional symbols of executive status and prioritizing practical solutions that benefit the entire organization, leaders can drive cultural change more effectively than through policies or pronouncements alone. The success of these initiatives demonstrates that when leaders truly embrace the changes they're asking others to make, resistance diminishes and adoption accelerates.

People Power:

I have come to believe that many organizations do not lack skills and capabilities with respect to their core competencies. This was truly the case with Gibraltar. They were thought leaders in the world of secure remote access and virtualization with many blue-chip clients. The challenge usually comes down to people and especially people not doing the right things.

When I arrived, Gibraltar's revenue was approximately 80% "non-recurring revenue" from hardware and software sales with approximately 20% from "recurring revenue" associated with professional and managed services. When valuing a company, a potential purchaser or investor is willing to pay a premium for a company with recurring revenue above one with non-recurring revenue. Accordingly, to maximize Gibraltar's value, our job was to significantly increase the recurring revenue component of the company's business.

The magnitude of the task ahead was daunting. It would require a change to compensation, sales capabilities, potential customers, and employee perception. This was a very tall order of change, and it reminded me of the quote:

"There is nothing more difficult to take in hand, more perilous to conduct, or more uncertain in its success than to take the lead in the introduction of a new order of things." Niccolò Machiavelli – Italian diplomat, philosopher & writer.

One of the other first things I implemented was the scorecard approach to people management that I had learned at TELUS and had scaled for smaller organizations through my time at NuTech. Part of this change was to create a vision for the company we wanted to be. This included a detailed description of how we wanted to move from software and hardware sales to professional and managed services. How we wanted to increase our recurring income to 40%, 60%, and eventually 80% over time. How we needed to obtain more clients for the services and how we needed to attract more people to staff our professional and managed services offerings.

The Art of Organizational Change: Finding the Right Pace

Leading significant organizational change is like trying to turn a large ship – push too hard or too fast and you risk capsizing; move too slowly and you might miss your window of opportunity entirely. The key lies in finding a measured acceleration, changes substantial enough to create meaningful impact but introduced at a pace that allows the organization to adapt and embrace them.

My approach involved developing a change management approach that balanced the need for significant transformation with the human capacity for adaptation. This meant carefully sequencing changes, celebrating early wins, and constantly reinforcing the connection between changes and positive outcomes.

It is also about consistency and persistence. If you are not relentless in helping to bring about the change you believe needs to be accomplished, the motivation for change can quickly dissipate.

The Call of Opportunity: When Past and Present Collide

The business world often creates interesting circumstances, and my situation at Gibraltar Solutions took an unexpected turn when my former partner, John O'Bryan, stepped into the role of Chairman at CBRE Canada. The timing was particularly interesting. CBRE had been steadily gaining market share since our departure from LePage, while our former employer had struggled to maintain its market position. John's appointment as Chairman was a strategic masterstroke by CBRE, leveraging his industry reputation and leadership capabilities to accelerate their growth.

At the same time, my experience at Gibraltar Solutions revealed significant blind spots in my perceived abilities and change management approach. Despite the company's promising progress, my eagerness to drive transformation led me to underestimate the nuances of evolving a founder-led organization. I failed to fully appreciate the underlying dynamics that had made the company successful in the first place.

My approach to organizational change proved inadequate. My execution lacked the patience and finesse required for such a delicate transformation. This humbling experience taught me that organizational change isn't just about having the right strategy – it's about having the wisdom to pace and scale the transformation appropriately. It was during this period of reflection that John O'Bryan approached me with an opportunity at CBRE. The timing was almost poetic; just as I was questioning whether I was the right fit at Gibraltar, a door opened to a different path. This situation perfectly illustrated a principle I'd learned throughout my career: sometimes the most significant opportunities arise when we're grappling with our current challenges.

The opportunity was a senior position in CBRE's integrated facilities management business. As CBRE continued to grow, they needed more senior level executives to assist in the growth and management of this people intensive business. CBRE had an immediate need for someone to manage a flagship account with a major Canadian bank. The opportunity that was presented to me was to come into the firm as the head of this account, which at the time had more than 300 CBRE team members. Once successful, I would then find my successor and ascend to the role of managing multiple accounts across Canada and part of the United States. There would also be opportunities for future development thereafter.

At Gibraltar, I truly loved the company's business prospects, the underlying technology, and the people. But my concerns about my ability to be successful twinned with the allure of working with John again caused me to accept the position with CBRE.

Being at the Heart of the Strategy: Lessons in Strategic Positioning

My experience at TELUS taught me a valuable lesson about organizational positioning that would influence all my future career decisions. While I successfully managed several substantial business units within TELUS, these divisions were ultimately peripheral to the company's core business and primary growth engines. Despite strong performance and recognition, I found myself on the outside looking in when it came to the company's strategic center.

This experience led to a fundamental shift in how I evaluated career opportunities. I came to understand that true organizational influence and career advancement often depend on being positioned at the heart of a company's strategic priorities.

This was my thinking with the opportunity at CBRE, where my leadership of the integrated facilities management business would place me near the center of the company's strategic growth. This division was particularly valuable because it generated recurring revenue – the holy grail for public companies seeking to improve their stock market valuations. The steady, predictable nature of this revenue stream made it strategically crucial to the organization's overall success.

The Power of Position: Negotiating from Strength

One of the most overlooked advantages in career negotiations is having a stable current position while exploring new opportunities. Throughout my career transitions, I've learned that the ability to walk away from a deal is often your strongest negotiating tool.

This principle proved particularly powerful during my negotiations with CBRE. What I didn't fully appreciate at the time was the strength of my negotiating position. The company had already presented several candidates to their major banking client, all of whom had been rejected. Unknown to me, they were feeling significant pressure to find the right candidate quickly. Adding to my advantage, several key decision-makers at the bank were former clients from my LePage days, providing a built-in level of trust and credibility that no other candidate could match. This situation created a powerful dynamic. I had a secure current position, CBRE had an urgent need, and I brought unique value through existing relationships with their key client.

This combination of circumstances allowed me to negotiate from a position of strength. I focused on securing not just attractive current compensation but also clearly defined terms for potential future scenarios, including termination provisions.

The experience reinforced a fundamental truth: the best time to look for a job is when you already have one. Not only does this provide financial security, but it also gives you the confidence and leverage to negotiate terms that truly reflect your value.

Leading by Example: The Power of Workspace Innovation

My commitment to leading by example continued at CBRE, where I again opted for a shared workspace model rather than the traditional executive office. The executive who hired me was surprised when I shunned the idea of a large private office in favor of a more powerful corporate computer. This decision wasn't just symbolic – it addressed a practical need for more meeting spaces while demonstrating a modern approach to workplace utilization. It also modeled our clients, many of whom were leaders in innovative workplace design. We needed to show we could "walk the talk."

Seeing Red

On arriving at CBRE, I knew that our banking client was not happy with our company's efforts. CBRE had a process through which their clients would rate the account teams in terms of their value to the client. This would be a version of the scorecard that I grew to embrace from TELUS. CBRE's scoring was red, yellow, green, and dark green, representing the range from bad to best. When I joined CBRE, our Canadian banking client deemed the account as red, meaning that they were dissatisfied with the efforts of CBRE.

The issue was fundamentally that we had incredibly well-intentioned people doing many things that were not deemed to be adding value to our client. Many people were doing what they believed was correct but falling short of the client's expectations. The other component of dissatisfaction was one of a lack of specificity. Goals were not measured specifically, and therefore what was delivered was interpreted very subjectively.

One of the first things that I introduced to the account team was the balanced scorecard performance objectives for the entire organization. We started with the leadership team and then cascaded the goals down to the lowest levels of the organization to bring about alignment. We also introduced a fifth tier of blue representing the highest level of achievement.

We made sure these goals had specific metrics around each of the levels of achievement. We then reviewed these metrics with our client to get alignment. This meant that there would be less subjectivity in performance as we moved forward.

The Power of Best Practices: Transforming Service Delivery Through Systematic Knowledge Sharing.

"Your mess for less" might be a cynical view of outsourcing, but the reality is more nuanced. When major organizations like Canadian banks outsource their real estate operations to firms like CBRE, they're seeking more than cost savings – they're buying into a promise of operational excellence through access to industry-wide best practices. The fundamental value proposition is straightforward: an outsourcing partner working with multiple large corporations should have accumulated a wealth of proven solutions and innovative approaches that can benefit all clients.

Our Canadian banking client highlighted a crucial gap in this promise. They observed that when problems arose, our teams often defaulted to creating custom solutions from scratch rather than leveraging existing knowledge from similar situations across CBRE's global platform. Their frustration was justified: "Surely some of your clients have already faced this situation. Why can't we benefit from their experiences?" This observation cut to the heart of the value proposition of outsourcing.

In the world of best practices, there's a critical distinction between importing practices (leveraging solutions from other clients) and exporting practices (sharing internally developed solutions with other clients). Clients typically see tremendous value in importing proven solutions but may perceive less benefit in exporting their own innovations. This created a clear mandate: become a net importer of best practices for our client.

The situation was particularly concerning given our team's size and prominence. With over 300 people, we managed one of CBRE's largest accounts globally, yet we barely registered in the company's "Best Practice Stars" recognition program. This underperformance in knowledge sharing indicated a systemic issue that needed addressing.

We approached this challenge using the Balanced Scorecard methodology, starting with the leadership team. We established clear, measurable objectives for both importing and exporting best practices, believing that a healthy balance would demonstrate both our ability to leverage CBRE's global platform and our team's capacity for innovation. Crucially, these goals were cascaded throughout the organization, making every team member responsible for contributing to our knowledge-sharing targets.

The results exceeded our expectations. Within months, our account team transformed from a non-entity in CBRE's best practice rankings to consistently placing in the top three globally. More importantly, we could demonstrate to our client tangible value from their outsourcing relationship through the regular implementation of proven solutions from CBRE's global platform.

The Power of Small Wins

This transformation, while focused on just one dimension of our service delivery, proved incredibly powerful for team morale. Many team members were discouraged by constant criticism and the account's "red zone" status. Success in best practice sharing became a catalyst for broader improvements, demonstrating that systematic change was possible through clear goals and consistent measurement.

This experience highlighted several key principles:

- Clear metrics drive behavior change.

- Individual accountability creates collective success.

- Small wins can trigger larger transformations.

- Systematic knowledge sharing creates measurable value.

- Performance measurement must align with strategic objectives.

This initiative demonstrated how the right combination of clear goals, systematic measurement, and individual accountability could transform an underperforming aspect of our service delivery into a source of pride and competitive advantage. It served as a foundation for broader improvements in our client relationship and team performance.

Your Toughest Clients: The Masters of Growth Through Adversity

"I am always willing to learn, but I don't often enjoy being taught" — Winston Churchill

Winston Churchill's quip about learning perfectly captures the challenging dynamic between service providers and demanding clients. Throughout my career, I've consistently found that your most challenging clients often become your greatest catalysts for growth, even if the process feels like an endless series of high-pressure at-bats with no easy pitches.

Our experience with the Canadian banking client exemplified this principle. As a sophisticated organization with exacting standards, they viewed it as their responsibility to continuously push for better performance, never settling for "good enough." Their demanding nature wasn't about being difficult; it was about driving excellence. Every achievement was met with new challenges, every solution with higher expectations. The team often found this relentless pressure exhausting, particularly when our best efforts were met with the seemingly lukewarm assessment of being "no longer red" on performance metrics.

However, this apparently modest achievement – moving from "red" to "not red" – represented a significant transformation in our service delivery. I worked to help our team reframe this dynamic, encouraging them to see our demanding client not as an adversary but as a demanding coach pushing us toward excellence. Just as a top-tier baseball coach constantly pushes players to improve, never fully satisfied even with good performance, our banking client was forcing us to elevate our game continuously. Their refusal to accept the status quo, while challenging, was a gift: they were investing their time and energy in making us better.

This experience reinforced a crucial leadership lesson: the way we frame challenges significantly impacts how teams respond to them. By helping our team understand that demanding clients serve as catalysts for improvement rather than sources of frustration, we could transform a potentially demoralizing situation into a growth opportunity. The journey from "red" to "not red" became not just a metric improvement but a testament to our team's resilience and capacity for continuous improvement. In the end, our most demanding client helped us develop capabilities and standards that benefited our entire organization, proving that sometimes the toughest teachers provide the most valuable lessons.

The Next Level: Managing Multiple Client Relationships

My tenure with CBRE's Canadian banking account, while not complete, did set the account team on the right trajectory and led CBRE's senior leadership to action their plans for my advancement. They proposed moving me into a broader leadership role overseeing a dozen major accounts across Canada and the central United States, while transitioning the banking account to a successor I was grooming. This promotion aligned with CBRE's original plans when recruiting me, and the timing worked well as my designated successor had already earned the client's confidence.

The new role presented an exciting challenge: merging into relationships with diverse client organizations and their respective account teams. Our portfolio included government agencies, technology companies, automotive manufacturers, financial institutions, and insurance companies, each with unique needs and operational cultures. This diversity demanded a flexible leadership approach and deep understanding of various industry sectors.

Crisis Management and Personal Accountability

However, my transition took an unexpected turn when a crisis emerged with one of our major technology clients. Their Toronto data center, managed by a CBRE team, experienced a catastrophic power failure during an unusual rainstorm. Despite having extensive fail-safe procedures in place, our team's failure to follow established protocols resulted in a significant outage affecting the client's blue-chip customers and triggered substantial service level agreement penalties.

While our team responded quickly and took full responsibility, providing detailed analysis and future preventive measures, the damage to our client's confidence was severe. The international organization demanded changes, specifically requesting new account leadership. As the senior leader in Canada, I was tasked with personally taking over the account management role, a situation that, while unfortunate for the previous account manager, was necessary to rebuild client trust.

Building for the Future

The challenge now became two-fold: stabilizing the client relationship while simultaneously searching for my eventual replacement. Unlike my previous experience with the banking client, there was no obvious internal successor within the account team. This required a broader search within CBRE, eventually leading to the identification and careful recruitment of a highly capable individual from another part of the organization.

This situation highlighted several crucial leadership lessons:

- The importance of having succession plans in place, even if the existing leader is years away from transition.

- The need for senior leaders to be ready to step in during crises.

- The delicate balance between supporting team members and meeting client demands.

- The critical role of rebuilding trust after operational failures.

The experience also reinforced a key principle in client service businesses: sometimes maintaining relationships requires difficult personnel decisions, even when dealing with capable professionals who have simply lost client confidence. It's a reminder that leadership often involves making tough choices that prioritize long-term organizational success over short-term individual considerations.

Strategic Networking Through Community Leadership: The CivicAction Story

While I was involved in repairing our technology client relationship, a senior executive from our banking client invited me to join CivicAction's Race to Reduce initiative. At first, it appeared to be a straightforward request to support an important client relationship. However, this invitation would prove to be a masterclass in strategic networking and industry positioning.

The Initiative

Race to Reduce, launched in May 2011 by CivicAction and its Commercial Building Energy Leadership Council, aimed to achieve a 10% reduction in energy consumption across Toronto's commercial buildings by 2014. The timing was perfect. Commercial buildings accounted for 20% of the Greater Toronto Area's carbon emissions, 37% of electricity consumption, and 17% of natural gas usage. This made it a critical environmental initiative, but it also represented something else: a gathering of the most influential players in corporate real estate.

The Strategic Opportunity

What made this initiative particularly valuable from a business development perspective was its composition. The Commercial Building Energy Leadership Council included senior executives from:

- Major commercial landlords

- Large corporate tenants

- Key service providers

- Financial institutions

In essence, it was a who's who of corporate real estate – exactly the decision-makers and influencers crucial to CBRE's integrated facilities management business development efforts. Rather than trying to secure individual meetings with these executives, I now had regular, meaningful interaction with them in a collaborative, non-sales environment.

From Participant to Leader

The initiative gained remarkable traction, growing to include over 175 buildings representing 67 million square feet (more than 32%) of Toronto region's office space. As I became more involved, I was asked to co-chair the initiative, a position that further enhanced my visibility and credibility within the corporate real estate community. This leadership role provided a platform to demonstrate expertise, build relationships, and establish trust with potential clients in a non-threatening context.

The Results

The program exceeded its goals dramatically:

- Year 1: 2% reduction (double the target)

- Year 2: 9% reduction (triple the projected goal)

- Equivalent to removing 3,598 cars from the road

But the real results were in relationship building. My involvement with Race to Reduce:

- Elevated my profile in the corporate real estate community

- Created natural opportunities for business discussions

- Built credibility through environmental leadership

- Established relationships with key decision-makers

- Positioned CBRE as a thought leader in sustainable facility management

This experience perfectly demonstrated how strategic community involvement can create powerful business development opportunities. By contributing to a meaningful environmental initiative, I was able to build relationships that would have been difficult to establish through traditional business development efforts. It reinforced a crucial lesson about networking: sometimes the most effective business development happens when you're focused on creating value for the broader community rather than pursuing immediate business opportunities.

The Challenge of Growth: Navigating Cross-Border Business Development

After successfully stabilizing the technology account and transitioning it to new leadership, I refocused on supporting our existing portfolio while pursuing growth opportunities. In an organization of CBRE's scale, new business development, particularly in the outsourcing space, follows a highly structured process. This included a dedicated pursuit team specialized in responding to RFPs (Requests for Proposals) from major organizations considering either first-time outsourcing or rebidding existing contracts.

The Cultural Divide

However, we soon encountered a significant challenge that proved a valuable lesson in cross-border business development. While CBRE's American pursuit team was highly skilled and experienced, their approach often failed to resonate with Canadian organizations, particularly government agencies. The nuances of Canadian business culture, from communication styles to decision-making processes to relationship building, differed substantially from the American approach. What worked brilliantly south of the border often fell flat in Canadian boardrooms.

This cultural challenge became particularly evident as we pursued several high-profile opportunities. Despite investing considerable resources – both in terms of time and senior executive involvement – and having strong technical solutions and competitive pricing, we consistently fell short in securing these major contracts.

In one high profile pursuit, I even went so far as to offer to step down from my regional management role to serve as the account leader of the new account. While this was seen as a significant advantage by the senior leader of the client account we wanted to win, the corporate decision was ultimately made higher up. They chose the incumbent service provider. It was a devastating loss.

The Winds of Change: When Corporate Transitions Lead to Personal Ones

One of the most important lessons in corporate life is that the relationships and agreements that brought you into an organization may not survive leadership changes. I was recruited to CBRE during a specific period when the organization needed a senior leader to stabilize their major banking relationship and drive growth. The executives who championed my recruitment and subsequent development had a clear vision for my role and trajectory within the organization. However, as is often the case in large corporations, leadership changes created new dynamics and different priorities.

New leaders brought new perspectives, priorities, and their own trusted networks. While this is a natural part of corporate evolution, it can leave executives who were brought in under previous regimes vulnerable to changing winds.

Looking back, the signs of this shifting landscape were visible, but I was deeply engaged in my work and I missed the subtle indicators of organizational change. While the disappointing losses of numerous client pitches were not entirely my fault, as the regional leader, I bore the responsibility for the results.

The Power of Preparation

This situation highlighted one of the most valuable lessons from my NuTech experience – the importance of having clear, written agreements, particularly regarding severance. This foresight proved invaluable when my new boss informed me of a restructuring that would eliminate my role. While the news was unexpected and disappointing, the clarity of my contract terms ensured a fair and professional transition.

The experience reinforced several crucial career lessons:

- Initial contract negotiations are crucial moments for protecting your interests.

- Political awareness is as important as operational excellence.

- The importance of maintaining external networks even when securely employed.

Bottom of the 8th Inning:

The eighth inning reflects a period when I saw opportunities to be an agent of transformative change at both Gibraltar and CBRE. At Gibraltar, the potential to evolve from a product-focused company to a service-led organization was clear. At CBRE, the opportunity to translate successful U.S. practices into the Canadian market seemed promising. In both cases, I envisioned a path to long-term success that required significant cultural and operational changes.

However, these experiences taught me the importance of the relationship between timing, organizational readiness, and personal ambition. The higher up the leadership tree you climb, the more exposed you become to the pressures of delivering short-term results while simultaneously driving long-term transformation. When immediate success proves elusive, the change agent often bears the burden, regardless of the validity of their long-term vision.

Looking back, I initially viewed these experiences through an intensely personal lens, focusing on what "should have" happened. Yet, with time and reflection, I've come to see them from multiple perspectives. The founders at Gibraltar weren't resistant to change – they were protecting a successful business they had built. CBRE's challenges in Canadian market penetration weren't about inadequate effort. They reflected the profound complexity of translating corporate cultures across borders.

Both experiences reinforced crucial lessons about organizational change and career management. Success requires more than just good strategies and strong leadership. The story serves as a powerful reminder that in business, as in baseball, knowing when to make a strategic change is as important as knowing how to implement it, and that personal career protection through proper documentation and agreements is essential regardless of performance level.

Having navigated multiple career transitions, from unexpected setbacks to strategic pivots, I understand the complexity of executive reinvention. If you're experiencing a career challenge, let's discuss how to transform it into your next opportunity. Schedule a confidential call at consistency-edge.com or download our Career Transition Readiness Checklist at www.consistency-edge.com/shop.

Key Takeaways:

1. The Timing Paradox

- Success often combines skill with serendipity

- "Perfect" strategies can fail due to timing

- Sometimes failure is a prelude to better opportunities

- Organizational readiness is as crucial as strategic vision

2. Cultural Transformation

- Cultural change requires both time and timing

- Resistance to change often masks valid concerns

- Evolution may be more effective than revolution

3. Leadership Perspective

- Multiple viewpoints exist in every situation

- Personal investment can cloud objective judgment
- Short-term pressures compete with long-term vision
- The higher the position, the greater the exposure

4. **Learning Through Experience**

- Success can be circumstantial
- Failure often teaches more than success
- Resilience builds through challenges
- The value lies in learning, not rationalizing

5. **Career Evolution**

- Closed doors often lead to better opportunities
- Perfect roles come at perfect times
- Professional growth requires perspective shifts
- Career paths rarely follow straight lines

These experiences, while challenging at the time, provided invaluable lessons that would prove crucial in future roles. They reinforced the principles of consistency while teaching new lessons about timing, perspective, and the complex interplay between personal ambition and organizational change. Most importantly, they set the stage for what would come next: a role at Sotheby's that would prove to be the perfect opportunity at the perfect time.

9th Inning

Finding Success in Unexpected Places: The Sotheby's Story

"Sometimes the detours are more interesting than the planned route." — Richard Branson

---

Learning Objectives:

After reading this chapter, you will:

- Understand how to transform perceived limitations into strategic advantages

- Learn to leverage corporate structure for competitive advantage

- Understand effective leadership of geographically dispersed teams

- Learn to use earned media for organizational impact

- Understand how to navigate corporate transitions

- Learn to build and maintain organizational cultures

Having just left CBRE, I found myself again activating my network for the next opportunity. This transition proved a powerful testament to many of the networking principles I've discussed earlier, particularly the importance of keeping an open mind and maintaining a consistent, professional approach even when immediate results aren't apparent.

The Power of Trusted Counsel and Open Minds

Once again, I launched my networking activities which were becoming old hat by now. Being strategic meant identifying who I wanted to meet with, having a very carefully crafted story about what I was looking for in the future, and an equally well-crafted script of who I was interested in connecting with.

During this time, my wife, Tanya, always an astute judge of opportunities, suggested I reach out to a successful entrepreneur friend of ours, Kerry Shapansky, who had largely stepped away from business to focus on philanthropy. Initially, I was skeptical. How could someone no longer active in business circles help my search? This hesitation reflected a common networking mistake: pre-judging the value of connections. Fortunately, I remembered the principle that networks work in mysterious ways, and I pursued the meeting.

Securing time with Kerry proved challenging, demonstrating another key networking principle – persistence. When we finally met, the contrast was striking: me in formal business attire, him casually dressed, a reminder that success often transcends superficial formalities.

Our conversation was engaging but ended with what seemed like a dead end: "You know, Brad, I've been out of the business world for a while. A lot of my former contacts are not current, and I'm really not sure how I can help you." I left our meeting convinced that I just experienced the 50% of networking that was wasted. Boy was I wrong.

The Unexpected Payoff

Weeks passed as I continued my disciplined networking approach, maintaining other connections and pursuing various leads. Then, unexpectedly, a text message arrived from Kerry. He had spoken with a recruiter seeking someone with my exact capabilities for a role in real estate. Without hesitation, he had recommended me. The role was for the President of Sotheby's International Realty Canada.

This experience perfectly illustrated several key networking principles I'd learned throughout my career:

1. The Power of Indirect Connections

Just as with my Gibraltar Solutions opportunity, the path to success wasn't direct. Networks often work through unexpected channels, creating opportunities through connections we might never anticipate.

2. Consistent Professional Approach

Even when meetings don't seem immediately fruitful, maintaining professionalism and making a strong impression can lead to future opportunities. Every interaction is a seed planted that might grow in unexpected ways.

3. The Role of Openness

Being receptive to meetings that might not have obvious immediate value can lead to surprising outcomes. This aligns with the principle of approaching networking as an information-gathering exercise rather than a direct job search.

This experience also validated the Consistency Effect in networking – success rarely comes from sporadic, intense efforts but rather from sustained, professional relationship building. Sometimes the most valuable connections come from seemingly unproductive meetings, and the most significant opportunities arise from unexpected sources.

So, embrace the chaos. Revel in the randomness. Think of networking like you're panning for gold in a river of small talk. You might have to sift through a lot of pebbles, but those golden nuggets are worth the effort. And even if half your networking efforts seem fruitless, you're still batting .500, which is not only impressive in baseball but would also make you a demigod in the world of weather forecasting.

Landing at Sotheby's: When Initial Skepticism Leads to Opportunity

When I first discussed the opportunity with the recruiter, my initial reaction was one of polite skepticism. While the Sotheby's brand carried undeniable prestige, stemming from its heritage as part of the legendary auction house, my perception of residential real estate brokerages (typically franchise operations where independent owners operated under a brand umbrella) made me hesitant. The prospect of managing brand compliance across multiple independent business owners, essentially leading through influence rather than direct authority, seemed like a step sideways rather than forward in my career trajectory.

However, the recruiter's persistence revealed a far more intriguing opportunity than first appeared. Sotheby's International Realty Canada (SIRC), she explained, wasn't a typical franchise operation but rather a wholly owned subsidiary of Dundee Corporation, a major Canadian success story founded by Ned Goodman. The role went far beyond managing the existing network of 32 offices and 500 sales professionals across Canada.

Dundee's strategic vision included re-entering the wealth management business, with SIRC playing a crucial component in this broader strategy. This revelation transformed the opportunity in my eyes. Instead of simply managing a luxury real estate brand, I would be participating in the ground-floor development of an integrated wealth management strategy, leveraging one of the world's most prestigious brands in the burgeoning high-net-worth sector. The chance to combine operational leadership of a national real estate organization with strategic involvement in wealth management represented exactly the kind of multifaceted challenge I sought. Naturally, having learned from past experiences, I ensured all aspects of this exciting opportunity were captured in a well-crafted employment agreement before signing on.

Building a Diverse and Distributed Leadership Team: The Power of Different Perspectives

Upon joining SIRC, I inherited a leadership structure that some might have viewed as challenging: a CFO and CMO in Vancouver, National Sales Manager in Montreal, and me in Toronto. When a Dundee executive questioned whether I planned to consolidate the leadership team in Toronto, I saw an opportunity to turn this geographic dispersion into a strength. A national company, I argued, should have leadership presence in its primary markets.

I learned to manage people I did not see every day at TELUS and CBRE. My teams were dispersed all over the world. This distributed leadership model has become increasingly relevant since the pandemic of 2020 transformed what was once an exception into a much more standard operating model, demanding specific skills and capabilities from leaders.

Managing remote teams successfully requires mastery of several critical competencies. First and foremost is the ability to foster genuine connection and trust without physical proximity. Leaders must develop heightened emotional intelligence to read virtual room dynamics and detect subtle signs of disengagement or conflict that might be more obvious in person. They need to master the art of virtual presence – maintaining authority and influence through a screen while remaining approachable and authentic.

Communication takes on new dimensions in a distributed environment as leaders must become experts at asynchronous communication, knowing when to use real-time interaction versus digital exchanges. Clear protocols need to be established for different types of communication, ensuring team members understand when to use email, chat, video calls, or other platforms. Moreover, they must develop the ability to convey complex ideas and emotional nuance effectively through digital channels.

This distributed leadership model also requires people to think differently. At Sotheby's, rather than investing in a prestigious Toronto office for myself, I advocated for redirecting those resources toward video conferencing technology across all our offices. This decision reflected three key principles of effective remote leadership: investing in enabling technology, prioritizing functionality over appearance, and demonstrating commitment to team connectivity.

The technology infrastructure decision went beyond mere video conferencing capability. It required robust digital collaboration tools, document sharing systems, standardized protocols for virtual meetings, and consistent access across locations. These systems became our digital workplace backbone.

This decision to invest in technology reflected both practical reality (I would be frequently traveling to our offices nationwide and did not really need a prestigious office) and strategic vision (creating infrastructure for better team communication and collaboration).

The choice of functionality over privilege and effectiveness over prestige resonated strongly with the team and set a tone for our organizational culture. More importantly, it established a framework for what would become essential leadership capabilities: creating inclusive virtual environments, maintaining team cohesion across distances, and building a strong organizational culture without physical proximity.

Success in this distributed model also required developing new performance management approaches. We established clear metrics and deliverables using the balanced scorecard approach while allowing for flexibility in work methods. Regular one-on-one virtual check-ins became crucial for maintaining alignment and providing support. We learned to balance autonomy with accountability, giving team members freedom in their work approach while maintaining clear expectations for results.

Embracing True Diversity

Our leadership team embodied multiple dimensions of diversity,not just in geography, but in perspective, experience, and background. Our team was split, 6 women and 5 men, with ages ranging from mid 30s to early 70s. Each team member contributed unique viewpoints shaped by their professional experiences and regional insights. This diversity proved particularly valuable in our decision-making processes.

My relationship with our CFO, Andrew Macfarlane, perfectly illustrated the value of diverse perspectives. As a classic CFO, his process-oriented, cost-focused approach often created tension with sales-driven initiatives. When others suggested replacing him with someone "more flexible," I reframed his role: "My job is to say yes, Andrew's job is to say no, and that healthy debate makes us stronger." While I could have overruled him, doing so would have diminished the valuable counterbalance he provided and potentially created a dangerous echo chamber.

Avoiding CEO Syndrome

This approach directly countered "CEO syndrome," meaning leaders surround themselves with yes-people, creating an environment where bad news or contradictory views are suppressed for fear of repercussions. By actively encouraging diverse viewpoints and healthy debate, we built a more robust decision-making process. If I couldn't convince our CFO of an investment's merit, it often prompted me to re-examine my own assumptions.

The success of this model demonstrated that true diversity – encompassing geography, gender, ethnicity, and, most importantly, diversity of thought – creates stronger organizations. By embracing different perspectives and encouraging open debate, we developed more comprehensive strategies and made better decisions. This experience reinforced that leadership isn't about having all the answers, but about creating an environment where diverse viewpoints can contribute to finding the best solutions.

Be Legendary: Elevating Every Client Experience

On my first day joining SIRC, I invited the two sales managers of the Toronto Central office to have lunch with me to establish our relationship and start the process of me understanding what was going on. Much to my surprise and delight, they said, "We would rather host a luncheon in our boardroom and invite salespeople to come and meet you." While I was enthusiastic to meet our people, what was I going to say after only a few hours at the company? Also, how many salespeople would come on comparatively short notice? I was shocked! It was standing room only in the boardroom. People had dropped whatever they were doing to come and see who this new CEO was and what his intentions were for the company. I had a lot more questions than answers and was more interested in listening than talking.

At that meeting, I encountered a surprising concern from our sales team. "Many people think we only do luxury real estate," they complained. "How do we convince them that we do all kinds of real estate?" This perspective caught me off guard. Our association with luxury, which I saw as a powerful market advantage, was being viewed as a limitation by many of our professionals.

Even more surprising was their proposed solution. Many salespeople wanted to create marketing materials that deliberately downplayed our unique positioning and prestigious heritage. They sought to "dumb down" our brand for more traditional real estate transactions, essentially stripping away the very elements that distinguished us in the marketplace.

When I pointed out that this approach would essentially erase everything that made us unique compared to our competitors, I was met with puzzled looks. The sales team hadn't considered that diluting our brand to appeal to a broader market might diminish our competitive advantage rather than enhance it.

This situation perfectly illustrates a common business paradox: the very attributes that make an organization special can sometimes feel like limitations to those working within it. The challenge wasn't to minimize our luxury positioning, but to help our team understand how our unique brand could add value to every transaction, regardless of price point.

The residential real estate brokerage business is fundamentally an independent business, with agents often viewing themselves as solo practitioners who succeed through their personal relationships with buyers and sellers. Many questioned whether brand association even mattered anymore. While they weren't entirely wrong about the importance of individual relationships, I saw an opportunity to change the industry's approach to luxury service.

Our strategy centered on a powerful yet simple premise: luxury isn't about price point – it's about experience. We crystallized this philosophy into our defining principle: "At Sotheby's International Realty, we believe that luxury is an experience, not a price, and that everyone who buys or sells a home deserves a luxurious experience." This became our rallying cry and the foundation for transforming the Sotheby's brand into a more inclusive, yet still prestigious, presence in the market.

To implement this vision, we drew inspiration from other luxury brands' success stories. Tiffany & Co., for example, delivers exceptional customer service regardless of purchase size. Whether someone is buying a modest charm or a magnificent diamond, the experience is consistently extraordinary. Every purchase receives the iconic Tiffany Blue box treatment, making each transaction memorable.

Even more inspiring was the Ritz-Carlton's approach to service excellence. A perfect example was their handling of a child's stuffed animal which was inadvertently left behind by a family that were staying at one of the hotels. Instead of simply returning it, the staff created a photo album documenting the toy's "extended vacation" at the hotel, showing it lounging by the pool, enjoying the spa, and exploring the property. This simple act of creativity transformed a potential disappointment into a legendary customer service story that enhanced the brand's reputation in the eyes of that guest and still does so today by the repetition of the story.

These examples became cornerstones of our inspirational sessions at Sotheby's International Realty Canada. We challenged ourselves daily to create our own "Ritz-Carlton moments" and deliver "Tiffany Blue box" experiences for every client, regardless of property value. This mindset shift permeated the organization, with every client interaction becoming an opportunity for exceptional service.

The results were remarkable. Client satisfaction soared, brand loyalty strengthened, and our team operated with renewed purpose and pride. Our agents began sharing their own extraordinary service stories, creating a positive feedback loop that reinforced our commitment to excellence. I began signing all communications with "Be Legendary" – not just as a slogan, but as a constant reminder to deliver exceptional service in every interaction.

This approach proved that true luxury in real estate isn't about property values; it's about creating meaningful experiences and lasting memories. In an era where technology threatens to depersonalize real estate transactions, we found a way to make them more human, more meaningful, and more impactful. We demonstrated that excellence in real estate isn't just about closing deals. It's about creating extraordinary experiences for every client.

The challenge remains relevant for anyone in any field: strive to be legendary in every interaction. When we pursue excellence in the everyday, we don't just elevate our performance – we transform lives.

The Power of Earned Media: How Sotheby's Unique Position Created National Impact

Brand Recognition and Market Position

While the Sotheby's auction house name carried immediate prestige worldwide, Sotheby's International Realty Canada was still establishing its presence in a market dominated by well-known brands like Royal LePage, ReMax, and Century 21. However, we possessed two unique advantages that would prove instrumental in building our brand: our corporate structure and our inherent association with luxury.

The Structural Advantage

Our organization of 32 corporate-owned offices across Canada stood in stark contrast to the traditional franchise model employed by our competitors. While other brands operated through a network of independent franchisees, each typically managing a small cluster of offices in specific geographic areas, we maintained unified corporate control across the country. This structure, unique in Canadian real estate, created opportunities that our competitors simply couldn't match.

The franchise model's limitations became particularly evident in media engagement. Franchise owners, naturally focused on their local markets, rarely had the ability or incentive to create messaging that resonated nationally. Their media coverage typically remained confined within municipal or provincial boundaries, making it difficult to build cohesive national brand awareness.

The Luxury Advantage

The market gifted us with a powerful advantage: our natural association with luxury through the Sotheby's auction house heritage. While we worked to make our brand more inclusive and accessible to all price points, our competitors faced the more challenging task of trying to establish luxury credentials from a mass-market position. As I often noted, it was easier to expand our brand downstream than for others to build credibility upstream in the luxury market.

This dynamic created an interesting paradox: while we were less known than our competitors in terms of general brand awareness, we enjoyed automatic credibility in the luxury space. Our challenge was to maintain this prestige while broadening our appeal, whereas our competitors had to maintain their mass-market presence while trying to establish luxury credentials – a more difficult balancing act.

Our unique corporate structure allowed us to manage this positioning consistently across the country, ensuring our brand message remained clear and cohesive from coast to coast. This unified approach, combined with our inherent luxury credentials, created a powerful platform for building national brand awareness through earned media, setting us apart in a fragmented market dominated by local franchises.

As President and CEO, I could speak authoritatively about luxury real estate trends across the entire Canadian market. There was no lack of media interest in luxury real estate.

This comprehensive national perspective made us particularly attractive to national media outlets seeking expert commentary on Canadian real estate trends, luxury markets, and foreign investment patterns.

We leveraged this advantage by regularly producing detailed market reports that analyzed trends in luxury real estate across multiple Canadian cities. These reports, backed by data from our nationwide network, provided valuable insights that our competitors, limited by their franchise structures, couldn't easily replicate. National media outlets increasingly turned to us as the authoritative voice on Canadian luxury real estate, particularly appreciating our ability to provide comparative analysis across different regions.

Earned media refers to publicity, coverage, or exposure that a company or individual receives through methods other than paid advertising. It's called "earned" because you earn it through newsworthy activities, expertise, or accomplishments rather than simply paying for it. Examples of Earned Media include:

- News coverage
- Television interviews
- Newspaper articles
- Industry publication features
- Expert commentary opportunities
- Social media shares and mentions

The value of earned media became evident as we gained regular coverage in prominent national publications like The Globe and Mail, National Post, and CBC News. In addition, I was a regular commentator on Canada's Television Bloomberg News Network (BBN). Our market reports and expert commentary featured in these outlets provided credibility that advertising simply couldn't buy. This media presence not only enhanced our brand awareness but also reinforced our position as thought leaders in Canadian real estate, particularly in the luxury segment.

Our unified corporate structure also allowed us to quickly respond to media opportunities and coordinate messaging across the country. Unlike franchise operations that needed to navigate multiple independent owners' perspectives, we could provide consistent, authoritative commentary on national trends while still maintaining deep local market knowledge through our regional offices.

This earned media strategy proved particularly valuable in building brand awareness among high-net-worth individuals who typically consume business and financial news. By establishing ourselves as the go-to source for insights on luxury real estate trends, we strengthened our position in this crucial market segment while simultaneously raising our profile among all potential clients.

Leveraging Unique Strengths: Creating National Impact from the CEO's Office

As President and CEO overseeing 32 offices and 500 sales professionals across Canada, I quickly recognized that our earned media strategy could become our most powerful tool for organizational impact. While larger franchised competitors had more offices and agents overall, their decentralized structure limited their ability to present a unified national voice. We had a unique advantage that allowed us to punch well above our weight in terms of market presence and brand awareness.

The mathematics of leadership impact was compelling: How could one person most effectively influence 500 professionals spread across a country as vast as Canada? Traditional approaches like office visits, while valuable, could only reach a limited number of people at a time. However, appearing on television or being quoted in The Globe & Mail could reach every agent, staff member, and client simultaneously, while enhancing our brand's credibility in every market we served.

This strategy created a powerful virtuous cycle. Each media appearance strengthened our credibility, which led to more media opportunities, further enhancing our national presence. Our agents and staff took immense pride in seeing their organization represented in national media outlets, and this pride translated directly into increased confidence in client interactions. Walking into a listing presentation shortly after being quoted in a national newspaper about luxury real estate trends gave our professionals a significant competitive advantage, regardless of their local market size.

The impact was particularly powerful because it benefited everyone in the organization simultaneously. When I would visit offices across the country, agents would frequently mention recent media appearances and how these had helped them in their business development efforts. They felt part of something bigger: a truly national organization with a powerful voice in the industry. This sense of pride and belonging helped create a stronger corporate culture and increased loyalty to the brand.

Moreover, this approach demonstrated how smaller organizations can compete effectively against larger rivals by identifying and exploiting their unique advantages. Rather than trying to match our larger competitors' marketing budgets or office count, we leveraged our structural advantage – unified corporate ownership and leadership – to create outsized impact through earned media. It was a perfect example of how strategic thinking and clear understanding of organizational strengths can level the playing field, allowing smaller players to compete effectively against much larger organizations.

The success of this strategy reinforced a crucial business lesson: sometimes your greatest advantages come not from trying to match competitors' strengths, but from recognizing and leveraging what makes your organization unique. By using national media as a platform, we could turn our comparatively smaller size into an advantage, creating a coordinated, powerful voice that resonated across the country and provided value to every member of our organization simultaneously.

The Power of Digital Leadership: Extending Personal Reach Through Video

As CEO of SIRC, I found tremendous energy in visiting our offices across the country. These in-person interactions provided invaluable opportunities to share our vision, explain our brand strategy, and engage with our people directly. However, the practical constraints of time, cost, and logistics meant that these visits, while valuable, couldn't provide the consistent, broad-reaching communication our organization needed. Monthly newsletters helped bridge the gap, but written communication alone couldn't capture the enthusiasm and personal connection that face-to-face meetings generated.

The solution emerged through what we called "Bradcasts" – regular video messages running 3-5 minutes in length. Working with our CMO, we developed short impactful communications to extend leadership presence across our national network. Like many initiatives that push us outside our comfort zone, self-doubt initially created hesitation. Would people find them hokey? Would anyone actually watch them? Would the effort justify the results? Pushing through these limiting beliefs proved to be one of the best decisions of my tenure.

The impact of these video messages exceeded my expectations in ways we hadn't anticipated. They reached team members who rarely had the opportunity for direct interaction with senior leadership, democratizing access to the CEO's perspective and vision. The videos reinforced messages delivered during in-person visits, creating a consistent narrative thread throughout the organization. Perhaps most importantly, they became part of our corporate culture, providing a regular touchpoint that connected our dispersed teams and reinforced our shared values and goals.

The success of the Bradcasts demonstrated a crucial lesson about modern leadership: digital tools, when used authentically, can create genuine connections and engagement across large, geographically dispersed organizations. They proved particularly valuable for recruitment, as potential team members could get a direct sense of our leadership style and corporate culture.

The videos also created a lasting library of content that new team members could access, helping to maintain consistency in our messaging and cultural orientation.

This initiative reinforced that sometimes the most impactful leadership tools are those that initially make us most uncomfortable. By pushing beyond traditional communication methods and embracing new formats, we created a more connected, engaged organization that better reflected our national presence and shared vision.

The Power of Purpose: Turning Mental Health Awareness into Collective Action

My involvement with CivicAction through CBRE led me to confront an issue I knew little about but would prove transformative for our organization: mental health in the workplace. While work-life balance had been part of my leadership vocabulary since my TELUS days, the depth and breadth of workplace mental health challenges were eye-opening.

Research from the Mental Health Commission of Canada reveals that one in five Canadians experiences a mental health problem or illness each year, with the economic burden estimated at over $50 billion annually. The stigma surrounding mental health makes it particularly insidious. It's often called the "invisible illness" in corporate settings, with many employees suffering in silence rather than risking career implications by seeking help.

At SIRC, we faced a unique challenge: how could a smaller organization without extensive HR resources make a meaningful impact in this space? While our larger corporate counterparts could implement comprehensive mental health programs, we needed to think differently. The solution emerged from understanding our unique strength – our network of successful sales professionals who had both the means and, as we would discover, the motivation to contribute to this cause.

The Response That Changed Everything

When I first introduced the concept of mental health awareness through one of my regular video messages to our national team, I was admittedly uncertain about the response. What followed was nothing short of extraordinary. The floodgates opened with emails, phone calls, and personal visits from team members sharing their own mental health journeys or those of family members. This overwhelming response not only validated our initiative but transformed it from a corporate program into a deeply personal mission for our organization.

From Awareness to Action

This groundswell of support led to a concrete initiative with Kids Health Links, focusing on children in long-term care facilities and Toronto's Internationally acclaimed SickKids Hospital. The project perfectly aligned our real estate expertise (helping people find homes) with supporting children who needed to feel at home in hospital settings.

Our pilot program in the Greater Toronto Area mobilized approximately 50 team members to assemble craft kits, helping hospitalized children personalize their spaces. The company matched fundraising efforts, with the top fundraisers earning the opportunity to personally deliver the kits to the hospital.

The impact was multi-faceted:

- Team Building: The project brought together professionals from across our offices, creating bonds beyond business relationships

- Community Impact: We provided tangible support to children in challenging circumstances

- Corporate Culture: The initiative demonstrated that even smaller organizations could create meaningful social impact

- Employee Engagement: Team members saw their company as not only an employer, but as a force for positive change

This experience proved that small companies can indeed think big when it comes to social impact. By leveraging our unique strengths – in our case, a network of successful professionals with the capacity and desire to give back – we created a program that benefited both our community and our corporate culture. The initiative demonstrated that meaningful corporate social responsibility doesn't require massive resources, just creative thinking and genuine commitment.

Corporate Pivots: Navigating Sale, Secrecy, and Personal Transition

The impact of leadership changes at the corporate level often creates ripple effects throughout an organization's subsidiaries, a reality I experienced firsthand at Sotheby's International Realty Canada. In 2018, when Jonathan Goodman succeeded his brother David as CEO of Dundee Corporation, it marked the beginning of a significant strategic shift. Within months, Jonathan made the decisive call to abandon Dundee's pursuit of a wealth management strategy, making Sotheby's International Realty Canada a non-core asset destined for sale.

This decision placed me in a particularly complex position that required careful balance of multiple responsibilities. As CEO, my primary allegiance was to Dundee Corporation. They were the sole shareholder and my employer, and their strategic decision to divest was entirely appropriate given their shift away from wealth management. My role became multi-faceted: assist in identifying potential buyers, negotiate the maximum sale price for Dundee, maintain stability within the organization, and navigate my own professional future.

Peerage Realty Partners, a subsidiary of Peerage Capital, emerged as the logical potential buyer.

Their mandate to acquire select residential real estate brokerages made Sotheby's an attractive target, though it would be significantly larger than their previous acquisitions. This situation created a delicate balancing act for me personally: while representing Dundee's interests in maximizing the sale value, I was simultaneously considering the possibility of continuing as CEO under Peerage ownership. This dual position required careful navigation to avoid any conflicts of interest while maintaining professional integrity throughout the negotiations.

For months, these discussions proceeded under strict confidentiality. News of a potential corporate sale can create significant anxiety among employees, potentially leading to departures of key personnel and disruption of business operations. Maintaining secrecy until we had certainty about the outcome was crucial for organizational stability.

After months of negotiation, Peerage Realty and Dundee reached an agreement on the purchase. However, Peerage's decision to install their own CEO to fully integrate the organization into their model meant another career transition for me. This situation once again validated the importance of clear, well-crafted employment agreements, a lesson learned from previous experiences. The careful attention I had paid to termination provisions in my original agreement with Dundee proved invaluable, ensuring I was treated fairly in the transition.

This experience reinforced several key leadership lessons about managing corporate transitions: the importance of maintaining confidentiality while preparing for change, the challenge of balancing multiple stakeholder interests, and the critical value of proper employment agreements. It also demonstrated how senior executives must often navigate complex situations where corporate interests, personal career considerations, and professional integrity intersect in challenging ways.

Legacy and Letting Go: The Emotional Side of Leadership Transitions

Professional transitions often carry emotional weight that business case studies rarely capture. My departure from SIRC was particularly poignant because of the deep connection I had developed with the organization. From the moment I joined, the prestigious Sotheby's brand resonated with my vision for luxury service, but it was the people who truly made the experience extraordinary. Over time, what began as professional relationships with our executive leadership team, sales managers, agents, and staff evolved into genuine connections that transcended typical business associations.

The process of letting go proved more challenging than I anticipated. When you invest yourself fully in an organization – not just in terms of time and effort, but emotionally and creatively – separation becomes more than just a career move; it's a profound personal transition. While I remembered my lessons from LePage, and deliberately tried not to let my personal identity become inseparable from my position as CEO, there is no doubt that a piece of me was left behind.

I had championed the "Be Legendary" philosophy, worked to transform our corporate culture, and witnessed the organization's growth from both a business and human perspective. Also, one of my significant contributions that was not totally recognized at the time was my insistence on getting our offices fully connected through video conferencing. While all of this happened prior to Covid pandemic, there is no greater gift that I could have left the organization than being prepared for the lockdown to come.

The enduring friendships and continued connections with team members across the country serve as a testament to the genuine community we built together.

While my tenure as CEO concluded, the impact of our shared accomplishments and the strength of these relationships remain as lasting legacies of my time with the organization. This experience reinforced a crucial leadership lesson: true success isn't just measured in business metrics, but in the lasting positive impact you have on people's lives and careers.

The Consistency Effect and GRAND SLAM in Action: A Sotheby's Story

At Sotheby's, the power of consistent, deliberate actions – rather than dramatic home runs – created transformative success. Let's examine how this experience embodied both the Consistency Effect and the GRAND SLAM framework:

Singles and Doubles That Built Success

- Reframing luxury as an experience, not a price point.

- Consistent earned media presence.

- Regular "Bradcast" video communications.

- Community engagement through charitable initiatives.

- Distributed and connected leadership across markets.

Each of these initiatives, while not spectacular in isolation, combined to create significant organizational impact. Like a baseball team that wins through steady base hits rather than occasional home runs, our success came from consistent execution across multiple fronts.

The GRAND SLAM Elements at Work
(only the most important elements)

Great Idea

- Each of the above ideas combined to be a great idea.

Resilience

- Persisting through initial skepticism and challenges with technology adoption.

Ambition

- Expanding beyond traditional luxury market boundaries

- Building national brand presence.

- Creating new standards for client service.

Network

- Finding the Sotheby's opportunity through indirect connections.

- Creating a "Best Practice" mentality across dispersed offices – globally.

- Building community through charitable initiatives.

Discipline

- Using our strength to combat competitors' strengths.

- Regular communications.

- Systematic media engagement.

Luck

- Being open to the opportunity with Sotheby's when it came along.

Action

- Taking action despite my own hesitancy.

These components of GRAND SLAM contributed to success, but it was their consistent application–- the steady accumulation of small wins – that created lasting impact. This experience perfectly illustrated that sustainable success comes not from occasional brilliant moves but from the disciplined execution of sound strategies over time.

Bottom of the 9th Inning:

The Sotheby's International Realty Canada story demonstrates the power of consistent, deliberate actions combined with strategic thinking. Through the steady accumulation of "singles and doubles" – from redefining luxury to building national media presence – we created transformative change.
It also demonstrates how understanding and leveraging your organization's unique characteristics can create competitive advantage. From transforming a perceived weakness (smaller size compared to competitors) into a strength through unified corporate messaging to redefining luxury as an experience rather than a price point, the journey illustrates the power of strategic thinking and consistent execution. The experience also highlights how authentic leadership, supported by innovative communication approaches and a commitment to inclusive culture, can transform organizations. Even when external factors lead to change, the lasting impact of strong organizational culture and clear strategic vision creates enduring value.

Key Takeaways:

1. Strategic Positioning

- Transform perceived limitations into advantages.
- Leverage organizational structure for competitive edge.
- Create consistent national messaging.
- Build on inherent brand strengths.

2. Leadership Communication

- Use multiple channels to reach dispersed teams.
- Embrace digital tools for consistent messaging.
- Make leadership accessible across the organization.
- Maintain authentic personal connection at scale.

3. Brand Development

- Define clear, inclusive brand positioning.
- Leverage earned media effectively.

- Create consistent national presence.

- Build on existing brand equity.

4. Organizational Culture

- Embrace diverse perspectives and locations.

- Build genuine connections across distance.

- Create shared purpose and values.

- Maintain culture through transitions.

5. Change Management

- Navigate corporate transitions professionally.

- Maintain confidentiality during changes.

- Balance multiple stakeholder interests.

- Ensure proper protection through documentation.

6. The Consistency Effect in Action

- Success through systematic, deliberate actions.

- Power of consistent execution across multiple initiatives.

- Importance of steady progress over dramatic changes.

- Value of integrated approach to organizational development.

These lessons demonstrate that organizational success comes from understanding and leveraging unique strengths while building authentic connections and maintaining professional standards through all phases of corporate life.

10th Inning:

The Leadership Trinity: Focus, Strategy, and Culture

"The essence of strategy is choosing what not to do."
— Michael Porter

Learning Objectives:

After reading this chapter, you will:

- Understand how productive anxiety serves as an indicator of strategic focus

- Learn to leverage the interaction between focus, strategy, and culture.

- Master the art of strategic clarity and decision-making

- Understand how to build and maintain cultural alignment

- Learn to evaluate opportunities through strategic and cultural lenses

- Recognize the power of collective strategic consciousness

- Master the orchestration of organizational elements for sustained success

In the game of baseball, there are traditionally 9 innings. Occasionally, when the score is tied, the game will go into extra innings. While we are not necessarily keeping score in this story, we are going to go into extra innings, starting with this one.

In the landscape of organizational leadership, three elements form a powerful trinity that determines success: the discipline of focus, the clarity of strategy, and the force of culture. While each is powerful on its own, their true strength emerges when they work in harmony. This interplay became clear to me through experiences at multiple organizations, especially during the period from TELUS to Sotheby's International Realty Canada, where the alignment of these elements created extraordinary results.

The Power of Productive Anxiety

One of my mentors shared a perspective that initially seemed mind boggling: "If you're not inherently anxious about what you're not doing, you're not focused enough." While grammatically awkward, this statement captures a fundamental truth about effective leadership – the relationship between focus, anxiety, and achievement. This productive anxiety, far from being a weakness, serves as a powerful indicator that you're maintaining proper focus.

As leaders, we face constant bombardment with opportunities, challenges, and demands for our attention. The natural tendency is to tackle everything, to be all things to all people. This approach, while well-intentioned, often leads to diluted effort and mediocre results across multiple initiatives rather than excellence in what truly matters.

The ability to maintain focus despite this discomfort separates exceptional leaders from average ones. It requires the courage to say no to good opportunities so you can say yes to great ones. It demands the discipline to keep your organization focused on key priorities even when other interesting possibilities arise.

Celebrating Strategic Anxiety

The discomfort we feel about unaddressed opportunities shouldn't be viewed as a negative emotion but rather embraced as evidence of effective leadership. This strategic anxiety signals that you've made deliberate choices with full awareness of their opportunity costs, maintaining the disciplined focus necessary for exceptional results.

Strategic Focus and Clarity: The Framework for Success

The fundamental purpose of strategy isn't just to define what you will do; it's to provide a clear framework for what you won't do. This clarity becomes the north star that guides decision-making at every level of the organization. When everyone understands the strategic direction, they can more easily evaluate how their activities and potential initiatives align with organizational goals.

The Strategy-Opportunity Paradox

There's a common saying in business that "opportunity shouldn't drive strategy." However, this requires nuance. While opportunities can accelerate strategy, they should never define it. I witnessed this principle in action while advising a CEO who faced an attractive acquisition opportunity outside his current geographic footprint. The target company was well-priced and profitable, seemingly representing an excellent growth opportunity. However, when examined through the lens of strategy, a different picture emerged. Geographic expansion wasn't part of the current strategic timelines, resources would be diverted from areas that would deliver stronger returns in existing markets, and pursuing the opportunity would ultimately dilute organizational focus.

The Power of Collective Strategic Consciousness

When strategy truly permeates an organization, something remarkable happens – the entire team becomes guardians of strategic integrity. This collective strategic consciousness creates alignment that goes beyond mere compliance to foster genuine organizational commitment.

I've witnessed this phenomenon across different organizations. At TELUS, the company motto "The Future is Friendly" evolved into a litmus test for decision-making at all levels. I remember a pivotal moment when a team member questioned a customer service approach by simply stating, "That doesn't sound future friendly." This observation demonstrated that strategy and values had become deeply embedded in the organization's DNA.

Similarly, at Sotheby's International Realty Canada, our "Be Legendary" philosophy took root in unexpected ways. When team members began critiquing management communications as not living up to our legendary standards, it was cause for celebration rather than concern. This feedback demonstrated that our strategic message had become a standard against which all actions were measured, including those of leadership.

Off-strategy opportunities, despite their surface appeal, extract significant hidden costs through diluted management attention and scattered resources that confuse organizational priorities. These diversions ultimately weaken strategic focus and diminish execution effectiveness across all initiatives.

Cultural Alignment and Amplification: The Force Multiplier

Peter Drucker's observation that "culture eats strategy for breakfast" isn't dismissing strategy's importance. It's recognizing that even the best strategy falters without a strong culture to support it. My experience at Sotheby's International Realty

Canada provided a powerful illustration of how culture can amplify strategic focus and transform organizational performance.

While strategy provides direction, culture provides the energy and alignment that powers exceptional execution. At Sotheby's, our culture wasn't just nice-to-have – it became our crucial differentiator. In an industry where core capabilities often look similar across competitors, culture became our tiebreaker in winning business and talent.

What made our culture unique wasn't uniformity – we were as diverse as the Canadian population we served. Rather, it was a shared passion for our brand and an uncanny ability to broker winning outcomes for customers, colleagues, and the company. This cultural strength manifested through several key dimensions:

Our mantra "luxury is an experience, not a price" wasn't just a tagline. It became our cultural foundation. Every team member understood that we weren't just selling homes; we were "artfully uniting extraordinary people with extraordinary homes." This sense of purpose infused every interaction, whether the property was modest or magnificent.

Values in Action

The Sotheby's culture stood on five essential values: delivering legendary customer experiences, fostering innovation through collaboration, leading our industry in integrity and professionalism, engaging with our communities, and committing to continuous growth. These principles guide every decision and interaction, creating our distinctive organizational identity.

The Strategic-Cultural Connection

While culture may eat strategy for breakfast, the real magic happens when they work in harmony. Our strategic focus on delivering exceptional experiences was amplified by a culture that celebrated exactly that kind of service.

This alignment created a virtuous cycle through which strategy provided direction, culture supplied energy, values guided behavior, and results reinforced our cultural foundation. Strong culture requires constant nurturing. As we grew, our leadership team remained vigilant about ensuring new team members would contribute positively to our culture. We understood that while no culture can overcome poor choices, a strong culture makes better choices more likely.

The TELUS Example: Integrating Focus, Strategy, and Culture

I had the opportunity to examine another example of aligned leadership at TELUS. Their approach offers a powerful demonstration of strategic focus implemented through clear alignment of purpose, priorities, and culture. Their carefully articulated strategic intent to "unleash the power of the internet to deliver the best solutions to Canadians" was operationalized through six specific strategic imperatives that created necessary boundaries while fostering productive anxiety about opportunities outside these parameters. This framework was further strengthened by deliberately chosen values – embracing change, passion for growth, spirited teamwork, and courage to innovate – that accelerated execution by shaping organizational behavior and decision-making at all levels.

What I took away from this experience is that strategic focus requires explicit mechanisms that connect high-level intent to daily decision-making. The most effective organizations create alignment between strategic imperatives and cultural values, establishing filters that maintain focus while acknowledging the inherent tension of declining opportunities outside strategic boundaries. When properly executed, this alignment creates a self-reinforcing cycle where strategic clarity drives focused execution, which delivers results that validate and strengthen the organization's strategic choices.

Bottom of the 10th Inning

Leadership excellence isn't about eliminating tension – it's about using it productively. It's not about doing everything – it's about doing the right things extraordinarily well. And it's not about perfect balance – it's about creative alignment of focus, strategy, and culture.

When leaders master this trinity of focus, strategy, and culture, they create organizations capable of consistent excellence in their chosen domains. In the end, it's not about managing each element perfectly – it's about orchestrating their interaction masterfully. That's where true leadership excellence emerges.

Key Takeaways:

1. Productive Anxiety

- Anxiety about unexplored opportunities indicates strong focus.

- Strategic tension is a feature, not a bug, of effective leadership.

- Clear choices create productive discomfort.

- Embrace anxiety as a compass for strategic direction.

2. Strategic clarity

- Strategy defines what you won't do as much as what you will.

- Opportunities should accelerate strategy, not define it.

- Clear frameworks enable consistent decision-making.

- Strategic intent must align with operational execution.

3. Cultural alignment

- Culture amplifies strategy when properly aligned.

- Strong culture makes better choices more likely.

- Cultural consciousness creates organizational guardianship.

- Values must support strategic imperatives.

4. Organizational Integration

- Focus, strategy, and culture form a virtuous cycle.

- Elements must reinforce rather than compete.

- Alignment creates sustainable competitive advantage.

- Integration matters more than individual element perfection.

5. Leadership Application

- Success requires orchestrating multiple elements.

- Tension between elements can be productive.

- Consistency in execution matters as much as design.

- Leadership excellence emerges from masterful integration.

11th Inning

The Power of Professional Friendships: When Career Paths Diverge and Reconnect

---

"In business, as in life, the strength of your network isn't measured by how many people you know, but by how many would help you when you need it most."
— *Robert Kiyosaki*

When Professional Relationships Transcend Roles: A Four-Decade Friendship

Life often teaches us that professional relationships can evolve into something far more meaningful than their initial context might suggest. In the early 1980s, what began as a simple hiring decision – bringing Randy Borron on as a research assistant at LePage – developed into a friendship spanning more than four decades and ultimately led to a rewarding chapter in my career.

During our initial decade together at LePage, our relationship evolved beyond the typical manager-employee dynamic. We discovered shared values, compatible work ethics, and mutual respect that transcended our professional roles. Even as we collaborated on business matters, we built a personal connection that proved more durable than any corporate affiliation.

The True Test of Professional Friendships

One of the most revealing moments in any executive's career comes not during their tenure at the top, but in the weeks and months after they leave an organization. It's then that you discover the true nature of what you thought were close professional relationships. The phone calls that once came daily suddenly stop, the lunch invitations disappear, and many of those who seemed like close colleagues fade into the background.

This phenomenon isn't surprising. Many professional relationships are role-based rather than authentic. When you're in a position of authority, people naturally gravitate toward you. Some of this is simple human nature; people want to be close to power and influence. The challenge is distinguishing between those who are drawn to your role and those who genuinely value you as a person.

I've experienced this transition multiple times throughout my career. Each departure served as a kind of friendship litmus test, revealing which relationships were role-based and which were genuine. It's a sobering experience to watch your once-busy calendar suddenly empty and your constantly-ringing phone fall silent.

Randy stood out as one of the rare exceptions. Our friendship, which began in a manager-employee relationship at LePage, transcended organizational charts and job titles. When I left LePage, it was a very emotional time for me since I had been there for nearly two decades and had much of my personal identity wrapped up in my job. While many other relationships faded, Randy remained a constant presence, checking in regularly, maintaining our connection, and sharing both professional insights and personal updates. Through my various career transitions across different industries and roles, our friendship remained steady and genuine.

This experience taught me valuable lessons about professional relationships. While titles and roles are temporary, authentic relationships built on mutual respect, shared values, and genuine connection can last a lifetime. In a business world often characterized by transactional relationships, these enduring friendships become increasingly precious, not just for their personal value, but for their ability to create unexpected opportunities for collaboration and growth later in our careers.

Contrasting Career Paths: Breadth versus Depth

When I left LePage, I pursued opportunities in other industries and our professional paths diverged dramatically, creating what I've come to see as a fascinating study in contrasting career strategies. While I embraced a broader path, exploring various industries and roles – from technology to telecommunications to residential real estate – Randy chose depth over breadth, staying within LePage (which eventually became Cushman & Wakefield) and building deep expertise in his chosen field.

Randy's career demonstrates the power of identifying and dominating a niche market. In the late 1990s, while most commercial real estate professionals focused on traditional office and industrial properties, he recognized an emerging opportunity in data centers. This insight proved prescient. As technology evolved and cloud computing emerged, data centers became increasingly crucial to global business infrastructure.

As one of the founders of Cushman & Wakefield's Global Data Center Advisory Group, Randy built a practice that differentiated itself from traditional real estate services. While the market segment was smaller than conventional sectors, it proved highly lucrative and faced significantly less competition. His team became recognized experts in this specialized field, handling complex requirements for major technology companies and financial institutions globally.

Coming Full Circle: Complementary Strengths

After leaving Sotheby's, Randy approached me about helping develop his team and assisting with the eventual transition of leadership to his son Michael. Our different journeys became a strength. My diverse experiences in leadership, real estate, technology, and team building across multiple industries complemented Randy's deep expertise in commercial real estate and data centers. What might have seemed like divergent paths created a powerful combination when brought together again.

The challenge was multifaceted. We needed to develop systems that enhanced standardized processes for complex transactions, implemented comprehensive documentation protocols, established quality control measures, and created consistent client communication frameworks. We clarified team member responsibilities and established performance metrics. Our marketing efforts included standardizing presentation materials, enhancing market research capabilities, developing thought leadership content, and building public relations strategies.

This experience validated many team-building principles while providing practical insights into their implementation. Documentation preserves expertise. Systems enable replication. Mentoring builds leadership. Planning ensures continuity. Development builds capability. Relationships transfer smoothly.

After five years, with systems in place, processes documented, and next-generation leadership established, it was time for my role to conclude. This experience demonstrated that while building effective teams is challenging, a systematic approach combining research, process development, and careful implementation can create sustainable success and enable smooth generational transition.

The fact that Randy and I would eventually work together again, decades after our initial relationship, stands as testament to the power of authentic professional friendships. It's a reminder that in business, as in life, investing in genuine relationships rather than role-based connections creates the foundation for both personal fulfillment and professional opportunity. It also proved that sometimes the most satisfying chapters in our careers come through relationships cultivated decades earlier.

12th Inning

Beyond Balance:
The Evolution of Work-Life Integration

"We don't need work-life balance; we need work-life harmony. Integration, not compartmentalization, is the path to wholeness." — Jeff Bezos

---

Learning Objectives:

After reading this chapter, you will:

- Recognize the limitations of traditional work-life balance approaches

- Learn strategies for effective work-life integration

- Recognize blind spots in career development

- Learn to identify and address self-imposed limitations

- Understand how happiness and fulfillment relate to work-life integration

- Master the art of strategic life planning

- Learn to balance experience acquisition with wealth accumulation

- Understand how to implement practical work-life integration strategies

- Understand how personal habits impact professional success

Beyond Balance: The Art of Work-Life Integration

The phrase "work-life balance" has become ubiquitous in corporate culture, suggesting that our professional and personal lives are opposing forces that need to be carefully weighed against each other. But this perspective may be fundamentally flawed. Instead of thinking about balance, which implies a zero-sum game where one area must decrease for another to increase, we should consider integration: the art of weaving our professional and personal lives together in a way that creates synergy rather than conflict.

The Balance Myth

I first heard the term work-life balance when I worked at TELUS. Until that point, my only guidance with respect to work-life balance was the credo "work hard – play hard." Like many large organizations, TELUS had a robust set of human resource programs.

The Evolution of Corporate Work-Life Programs: Promise vs. Reality

In the 1980s and 1990s, corporations introduced work-life balance programs with great fanfare. These initiatives typically included a standard package of offerings: flex-time arrangements that allowed for modified work hours, employee assistance programs providing counseling and support services, childcare referral networks (though rarely actual childcare facilities), basic wellness programs centered around annual health screenings, and remote work policies that existed primarily on paper. While these programs looked impressive in recruitment materials, their practical implementation often fell far short of their promised benefits.

The gap between promise and reality stemmed from deeply entrenched cultural resistance within organizations. Managers frequently viewed employees who utilized these programs as less committed to their careers, creating an environment where workers feared career penalties for participating. The traditional emphasis on "face time" remained firmly entrenched, with corporate culture continuing to reward long hours and physical presence in the office above actual productivity or results. This was certainly my experience at TELUS. This created a paradoxical situation where programs existed, but employees felt unsafe using them.

Perhaps most problematic were the mixed messages organizations sent about work-life balance. Companies would proudly promote their family-friendly policies while simultaneously maintaining expectations of constant availability and immediate responsiveness. Success stories within organizations typically celebrated workaholics who sacrificed personal life for professional achievement, rather than highlighting individuals who successfully balanced both spheres. Even technology, introduced as a tool for flexibility, often became a means of extending work hours into personal time.

These early attempts at work-life balance programs provide valuable lessons for modern organizations. First and foremost, they demonstrate that policies alone cannot change deeply ingrained cultural norms. Real change requires visible leadership commitment, with senior executives modeling the desired behaviors and actively supporting program utilization. Programs need genuine organizational support, including adequate resources, proper training for managers, and clear implementation guidelines. Most importantly, organizations must align their stated values with their actual practices, ensuring that employees who take advantage of work-life programs aren't inadvertently penalized for doing so.

The Evolution of Work-Life Integration: A Global Perspective

The traditional concept of work-life balance, with its rigid separation between professional and personal spheres, has become all but obsolete in our interconnected world. My experience at TELUS in the early 2000s provided a perfect lesson in why integration, rather than balance, offers a more practical approach to modern leadership.

As my responsibilities at TELUS expanded, so did the geographic spread of my teams. What began as managing local groups in Toronto evolved into overseeing teams across multiple Canadian time zones, eventually extending to international operations. This global reach meant that traditional 9-to-5 workdays became impractical, if not impossible. When you're managing teams from Manila to Toronto, someone's 9 AM is someone else's 9 PM.

This reality forced me to reconceptualize how I thought about work and personal time. Instead of trying to maintain strict boundaries between professional and personal hours, I began viewing my day as a fluid series of opportunities and responsibilities. If I needed to participate in a midnight conference call with our Asia Pacific operations, it made sense to handle personal matters during traditional business hours. While this approach initially triggered feelings of guilt – a common reaction shaped by industrial-era thinking about work – I gradually recognized that this flexibility wasn't just necessary but more effective. This philosophy has carried on through all of my future endeavors and even today in my coaching business.

Research supports this shift in thinking. A Harvard Business Review study found that employees who successfully integrate work and personal life report significantly higher job satisfaction and lower stress levels compared to those attempting strict separation. This makes intuitive sense. When we stop fighting against the natural overlap between our professional and personal lives, we can focus our energy on optimizing both rather than trying to keep them artificially separate.

Technology plays a crucial role in enabling this integration, but it must be managed thoughtfully. The same tools that allow us to connect with global teams can easily become instruments of constant interruption if not handled properly. The goal is to use technology to facilitate flexibility while maintaining boundaries that protect our well-being.

For leaders, modeling this integrated approach becomes particularly important. When team members see their leaders comfortably managing personal matters during traditional work hours and handling professional responsibilities during "off" hours, it helps normalize this more fluid approach to time management. This cultural shift is essential for creating an environment where true work-life integration can flourish.

Success in this paradigm isn't measured by how well we separate our professional and personal lives, but by how effectively we integrate them to create a sustainable and fulfilling lifestyle. The goal isn't perfect balance; it's purposeful integration that allows us to be fully present and effective in all aspects of our lives.

Moving Beyond Balance: The Power of Work-Life Integration

Successfully integrating work and personal life offers substantial benefits beyond traditional "balance" approaches. This integration reduces stress and anxiety while improving job satisfaction and enhancing family relationships. Research shows it contributes to better overall well-being, increased productivity, and greater career sustainability by creating natural synergies between professional and personal domains.

As remote and hybrid work arrangements become increasingly common, the integration approach gains relevance. The fundamental shift lies in recognizing that work and life aren't opposing forces requiring "balance," but complementary aspects of a fulfilling existence that can be thoughtfully integrated.

Work-Life Integration: Beyond Balance to Authentic Happiness

The pursuit of happiness in modern life often feels elusive, particularly for professionals striving to reconcile career success with personal fulfillment. Harvard happiness researcher Arthur Brooks offers a perspective that offers a new view on our understanding of both happiness and the relationship between work and personal life. Rather than viewing happiness as merely the presence of pleasure or absence of stress, Brooks suggests a more nuanced approach based on meaningful integration rather than artificial balance.

The Four Pillars of Authentic Happiness

Brooks identifies faith, family, friends, and work as the crucial elements for life satisfaction. Faith encompasses our core values and sense of purpose beyond any specific religious practice. Family and friends provide essential emotional foundations. Work offers opportunities for meaningful achievement and societal contribution. The key insight is that these elements function best not when perfectly balanced but when thoughtfully integrated.

The Happiness Misconception

Many professionals fall into the trap of believing extraordinary success in one area (typically work) will eventually create happiness across all domains. This misconception often leads to sacrificing personal relationships and well-being for professional achievement. I experienced this firsthand, constantly setting new business goals rather than celebrating achievements, perpetually defining happiness as something to be attained in the future. The fundamental flaw in this approach becomes clear when we recognize that consistent, meaningful engagement across all life domains creates greater satisfaction than exceptional achievement in just one area.

Creating Meaningful Integration

True happiness emerges from developing daily habits that incorporate all pillars of happiness rather than attempting to maintain artificial boundaries between them. Small, consistent actions across all areas yield greater satisfaction than sporadic grand gestures. This might include brief family check-ins throughout the workday, regular personal reflection, integrating social connections with professional networking, and choosing work projects that align with personal values.

Success Redefined

Viewed through this lens, success isn't about perfect balance or extraordinary accomplishments in isolated domains. Instead, it means creating a life where professional achievement, personal relationships, core values, and meaningful contributions naturally reinforce each other. This integrated approach leads to a more sustainable and satisfying life experience.

The goal shifts from achieving perfect equilibrium between competing priorities to creating a cohesive life where each element contributes to overall purpose and well-being.

A Wake-Up Call About Wealth

I spent decades pursuing financial success, working well into my 60s, focused almost exclusively on making money. Like many successful executives, I measured achievement by the size of my bank account. I was following the same path my father had taken: work hard, save diligently, and accumulate wealth for retirement.

But watching my father reach his 80s and 90s taught me a harsh lesson. Despite having significant financial resources, he lacked the energy and physical ability to enjoy them. His wealth, carefully accumulated over a lifetime, couldn't buy back the vitality needed for the experiences he had postponed.

Die with Zero?

Then I read Die with Zero by Bill Perkins, and it fundamentally changed my perspective. Perkins articulates what I had begun to understand through observation but hadn't fully processed: we have this backwards. The goal isn't to accumulate the maximum amount of wealth; it's to use our resources – time, energy, and money – when they can create the most meaningful impact in our lives.

This isn't about reckless spending or dying broke. It's about understanding that memories and experiences, not bank statements, provide comfort and satisfaction in our later years. Perkins challenged my deeply ingrained wealth accumulation mindset, showing me that optimizing life experiences matters more than maximizing financial returns. I wish I had understood this sooner, but it's a lesson worth sharing at any age.

Perkins outlines three distinct life stages that fundamentally shape our ability to accumulate and enjoy experiences. During the "Go-Go

Years," spanning our twenties through forties, we experience peak physical capabilities and energy levels. This period represents the optimal time for adventurous and physically demanding experiences. Ironically, this is also when most people defer experiences to focus on career building, missing their prime window for certain activities.

The "Slow-Go Years," from our fifties through seventies, typically bring increased financial resources but declining physical capabilities. This stage presents a critical window for moderate-intensity experiences. While we may have accumulated the means to pursue our dreams, our physical limitations begin to narrow the range of possible activities.

Finally, the "No-Go Years," occurring in our eighties and nineties, often feature abundant time and financial resources but significantly limited physical capabilities. During this stage, the focus necessarily shifts to relationships and less physically demanding experiences. This phase underscores Perkins' central argument: waiting too long to pursue experiences can mean missing them entirely, regardless of financial means.

This framework challenges the traditional retirement-focused life planning model, emphasizing that certain experiences must be prioritized during specific life stages, regardless of financial status. The key isn't just having the money to do something.It's having both the money and the physical capability when it matters most.

Bottom of the 12th Inning

The journey from traditional work-life balance to modern work-life integration reflects a fundamental shift in how we approach both career and personal fulfillment. Through examining the evolution of corporate programs, global workplace changes, insights from happiness research, and personal challenges – including the impact of social drinking culture – we see that true success lies not just in balancing competing demands but in making conscious choices that enhance both professional and personal life. The combination of Arthur Brooks' happiness research, Bill Perkins' "Die with Zero" philosophy, and honest self-reflection about our habits and choices provides a framework for creating a life rich in both achievements and experiences, free from self-imposed limitations.

Key Takeaways:

1. Historical Perspective

- Traditional work-life balance programs often fail due to cultural resistance.

- Early corporate initiatives provided structure but lacked practical support.

- Evolution of global work has necessitated new approaches to integration.

2. Integration vs. Balance

- Integration creates synergy rather than competition between life domains.

- Flexibility and adaptability are crucial for modern success.

- Technology enables integration but requires thoughtful management.

3. Personal Habits and Professional Success

- Recognize how social customs can become career limitations.

- Identify personal habits that may be impeding success.

- Acknowledge that it's never too late to make positive changes.

- Recognize how personal choices impact professional effectiveness.

- Understand that removing obstacles can be as important as adding achievements.

4. The Happiness Factor

- True fulfillment comes from meaningful engagement across multiple life domains.

- Faith, family, friends, and work form the pillars of lasting happiness.

- Consistent engagement beats sporadic achievement.

5. Strategic Life Planning

- Different life stages offer unique opportunities and limitations.

- Time and energy are more valuable than money alone.

- Experience planning should consider physical capabilities across decades.

- Creating memories is as important as accumulating wealth.

6. Implementation Strategies

- Create decade-by-decade experience and achievement plans.

- Prioritize time-sensitive experiences.

- Balance current enjoyment with future security.

- Focus on "return on experience" alongside financial returns.

13th Inning:

Dismantling the Roadblocks – Conquering the Barriers to Lasting Consistency

---

"It's not what we do once in a while that shapes our lives. It's what we do consistently." — Tony Robbins

---

Learning Objectives:

After reading this chapter, you will:

- Understand the common psychological, neurological, systemic, and accountability-related barriers that hinder consistent action.

- Recognize why preventative, consistent efforts are often undervalued compared to reactive, heroic interventions (The Prevention Paradox).

- Identify how inherent brain wiring (Neural Barriers) can prioritize short-term wins over long-term consistent gains.

- Learn how organizational structures and reward systems (Systemic Challenges) can inadvertently discourage consistency.

- Appreciate the impact of "Measurement Aversion" and the critical role of accountability in fostering consistency.

- Master practical strategies at both individual and organizational levels to overcome these barriers and cultivate lasting consistency.

In the preceding chapters, we've laid the groundwork for understanding *why* consistency is the veritable bedrock of enduring success. We've explored how the relentless pursuit of "singles and doubles," those seemingly modest but steadfast actions, inevitably outperforms the sporadic chase for "grand slams." The principles of "The Consistency Effect" are clear: sustained, deliberate effort, compounded over time, is the most reliable path to achieving what truly matters.

However, as many of us have experienced, knowing this truth and living it day-in and day-out are two different propositions. The path to consistent action is often littered with obstacles – some internal, some external, all potent enough to derail even the best intentions. It's one thing to appreciate the power of consistency; it's another entirely to weave it into the fabric of our personal habits and our organizational cultures.

We now turn our attention to these very roadblocks. We will dissect the common, yet often insidious, barriers that prevent individuals and organizations from harnessing the full power of "The Consistency Effect." More importantly, we will equip ourselves with practical, actionable strategies – the tools and mindsets needed not just to navigate these barriers, but to dismantle them, paving the way for consistency to become less of a struggle and more of an ingrained, almost automatic, way of operating.

Unmasking the Adversaries: The Common Saboteurs of Consistent Effort

If consistency is the engine of achievement, then these barriers are the grit in the gears. Recognizing them is the first step towards neutralizing their impact. In my years of observation and practice, four primary adversaries consistently emerge:

1. The Alluring Siren Song of the "Prevention Paradox"

As we've touched upon, our human psychology and, indeed, many organizational cultures, are strangely biased against the quiet heroism of prevention.

The consistent, often invisible work that *prevents* problems – the diligent fire marshal meticulously ensuring safety – rarely garners the applause reserved for the firefighter dramatically saving the day. Who gets the bigger bonus, the spotlight, the promotion? Often, it's the individual who swoops in to manage a crisis, not the one whose steady hand ensured no crisis erupted in the first place.

This "firefighter bias" is a core challenge to *The Consistency Effect*. It means that the daily discipline of incremental improvement, the consistent oiling of the machinery, the proactive addressing of minor issues – these vital 'singles' – struggle for recognition against the visible, often heroic narrative of transformational change or crisis intervention. This paradox subtly steers us away from the very behaviors that build long-term stability, rewarding reactive heroism over proactive consistency.

2. The Brain's Betrayal: Our Neural Hardwiring for the Quick Win

Beyond external validation, a significant challenge lies within our own minds. Neuroscience confirms that our brains are, in many ways, wired for immediate gratification. The release of dopamine, that "feel-good" neurotransmitter, is often more pronounced for immediate rewards than for those that are delayed and long-term. This biological tendency contributes powerfully to "present bias," where the allure of a quick win today overshadows the potentially greater, but more distant, benefits of sustained effort.

In the context of *The Consistency Effect*, this neural wiring is a formidable foe. Why diligently pursue a six-month process improvement that promises gradual gains when closing a quick deal *now* offers an immediate jolt of satisfaction and recognition? This internal pull towards the "grand slam" moment makes the patient, sometimes monotonous, work of consistency feel less appealing, even when our rational mind understands its superior long-term value.

3. The System's Snare: When Organizational Structures Reward Inconsistency

Even if we manage our internal biases, the very systems we operate within can actively undermine our best efforts towards consistency. Many organizational environments, as I've detailed in *The Consistency Effect*, are inadvertently designed to reward the wrong behaviors. Compensation structures, promotion criteria, and recognition programs are frequently geared towards dramatic, short-term results – the quarterly sprints, the splashy project launches, the rapid (and sometimes unsustainable) growth.

When the rules of the game reward high-stakes gambles and short-term heroics over reliable, steady performance, it creates a powerful disincentive for the consistent work that builds true, lasting value. Why invest in a meticulous, long-term customer relationship strategy (a series of 'doubles') if your bonus is tied exclusively to this month's sales figures (a potential 'home run' or 'strikeout')? These systemic challenges can make pursuing consistency feel not only difficult but professionally risky.

4. The Mirror's Glare: Our Aversion to Honest Measurement

Finally, a cornerstone of *The Consistency Effect* is accountability, and accountability demands measurement. To know if we are being consistent, to understand the impact of our steady efforts, we *must* measure our actions and their results over time. Yet, for many, this simple requirement triggers a significant internal resistance – what is called "measurement aversion."

This isn't necessarily about laziness; it's often about the discomfort of confronting potential shortcomings, the gap between our intentions and our actions, or the slow pace of incremental progress. We avoid the scale because we might not like the number it shows. Yet, as the adage goes, you cannot manage what you do not measure. Without honest, consistent tracking, we are flying blind, unable to make informed adjustments or truly appreciate the cumulative power of our efforts. This aversion is a direct impediment to embedding consistent practices.

Forging Your Consistency Armor: Systemic Solutions and Strategic Mindsets from "The Consistency Effect"

Understanding these adversaries is critical, but *The Consistency Effect* is ultimately a book about solutions – about building the "muscle" of consistency. The following strategies are designed to directly counter these barriers, creating an environment where consistent action becomes the path of least resistance and greatest reward.

1. Systematically Celebrating the "Singles and Doubles" to Counter Neural Bias and the Prevention Paradox

Since our brains crave immediate rewards and our cultures often overlook preventative work, we must intentionally create more frequent, positive feedback loops for consistent, value-building actions.

- At the Individual Level: Don't wait for the marathon to finish to celebrate. Acknowledge your daily or weekly adherence to your chosen consistent actions. Finished your planned writing for the day? Stuck to your new process for a whole week? Create small, immediate, personal rewards. This helps retrain your brain, associating consistency with positive reinforcement.

- At the Organizational Level: Implement a "Small Wins" Celebration System. Leaders must become champions of the "single and double." This means actively and publicly highlighting the small, consistent efforts that contribute to larger goals or prevent problems. Dedicate time in meetings to "Consistency Wins." Create visible recognition platforms (a "Consistency Wall of Fame," for instance) for teams or individuals who exemplify steady progress and reliable execution. As *The Consistency Effect* advocates, when these vital, often unseen, contributions are brought into the light and celebrated, their value is reinforced, and the culture begins to shift.

2. Redesigning Rewards and Standardizing Processes to Navigate Systemic Challenges

If the system rewards inconsistency, it's time to challenge and change the system.

- Introduce "Consistency Scorecards": This is a core tenet of operationalizing *The Consistency Effect*. Move beyond performance metrics that only capture outputs or "grand slams." Develop scorecards that explicitly track and reward adherence to key processes, proactive problem prevention, and steady, incremental improvements. A sales scorecard, for example, shouldn't just track closed deals; it should also measure consistent prospecting activities, CRM data integrity, and disciplined follow-up cadences. These scorecards make the process of achieving results as important as the results themselves, directly rewarding the consistent behaviors that lead to sustainable success. Co-create these with teams to ensure buy-in and relevance.

- Standardize Key Processes and Embed Them from Day One: *The Consistency Effect* champions the idea that well-defined processes are the architecture of consistent execution. They reduce ambiguity and ensure everyone is working from the same playbook. Invest in Standardized Onboarding and Continuous Training that focuses not just on what to do, but why specific processes are crucial for collective success. Explain how consistent adherence to these processes contributes to the company's overall strategy of hitting those reliable "singles and doubles."

3. **Making Measurement a Tool for Growth to Embrace Accountability and Counter Measurement Aversion**

Measurement should not be a source of fear, but a source of essential feedback – the compass that guides continuous improvement.

- At the Individual Level: Implement simple, sustainable tracking methods for your key consistent actions and goals. View the data not as a judgment, but as valuable information. Is your batting average improving? Are your on-base percentages climbing? This data shows the cumulative impact of your steady efforts and highlights areas for refinement.

- At the Organizational Level: Establish "Process Improvement Feedback Loops." This transforms measurement from a top-down mandate into a collaborative engine for growth. Create formal, accessible channels (regular review meetings, digital suggestion platforms) where employees who are living the processes daily can provide input on their effectiveness and efficiency. When people see their insights valued and acted upon, their engagement with processes deepens, and "measurement aversion" gives way to a sense of ownership and a desire for continuous improvement – a virtuous cycle that *The Consistency Effect* seeks to create.

4. Leading by Example and Cultivating Patience – The Long Game of Habit Formation

Consistency, like any valuable skill, takes time and deliberate practice to master.

- Give Consistency Time to Become a Habit: Remind yourself and your teams that building new, consistent habits is a marathon, not a sprint. Research, such as the Lally and colleagues' study, indicates it can take an average of 66 days for a new behavior to become automatic. The key is patient, persistent effort. *The Consistency Effect* itself is a testament to the power of long-term, sustained application.

- Champion "Walk the Talk" and Consistency Coaching: Leadership is paramount. Leaders must be the chief architects and role models of a consistency-driven culture. This means:

  - Personal Discipline: Demonstrating unwavering commitment to their own consistent habits and adherence to processes.

  - Consistent Communication: Relentlessly reinforcing the strategic importance of steady effort over sporadic heroics.

  - Protecting Consistent Efforts: Shielding teams focused on long-term, incremental improvements from the constant barrage of urgent, short-term demands.

  - Coaching for Consistency: Making it a regular part of performance discussions, helping individuals identify their own consistency challenges and develop strategies to overcome them.

The Unfolding Power of Embedded Consistency

The journey to instill deep-seated consistency, whether in our personal lives or across an entire organization, is not without its challenges. The barriers we've discussed are real and pervasive. Yet, by understanding them and by proactively implementing the strategies outlined – strategies rooted in the core philosophy of*The Consistency Effect* – we can systematically dismantle these roadblocks.

This isn't about achieving perfection overnight. It's about a steadfast commitment to the process, an unwavering belief in the compounding power of small, regular actions. It's about building an environment where hitting singles and doubles is not only valued but is understood as the most reliable way to win the game. As consistency becomes less of an effort and more of an ingrained reflex, its transformative power truly begins to unfold, leading to the kind of robust, sustainable, and deeply rewarding success that *The Consistency Effect* promises.

Bottom of the 13th Inning

This chapter has illuminated the common yet formidable roadblocks that prevent individuals and organizations from fully harnessing the power of consistency. We've dissected the "Prevention Paradox," the brain's bias for "Quick Wins," the "System's Snare" of misaligned rewards, and the "Mirror's Glare" of measurement aversion. More importantly, we've equipped ourselves with actionable strategies—from systematically celebrating small wins and redesigning reward systems to embracing measurement as a growth tool and leading by example—to dismantle these barriers. The journey to embedded consistency is about a steadfast commitment to the process, transforming consistent action from a struggle into an ingrained reflex, thereby unlocking the robust, sustainable, and deeply rewarding success promised by *The Consistency Effect.*

Key Takeaways:

1. Understanding the Barriers to Consistency

- Prevention Paradox: Recognize that consistent, preventative work is often less visible and rewarded than dramatic crisis management.

- Neural Barriers: Understand that our brains are often wired for immediate gratification, making sustained, long-term effort less appealing.

- Systemic Challenges: Identify how organizational structures (e.g., compensation, promotions) can inadvertently reward short-term results over consistent performance.

- Measurement Aversion: Acknowledge the common resistance to tracking progress due to fear of confronting shortcomings, despite its necessity for improvement.

2. Strategies for Overcoming Psychological & Neural Barriers

- Celebrate Small Wins: Implement systems to acknowledge and reward incremental progress ("singles and doubles") to create positive feedback loops.

- Individual Rewards: Encourage personal, immediate rewards for consistent daily/ weekly actions to retrain brain associations.

- Organizational Recognition: Dedicate time and platforms (e.g., "Consistency Wall of Fame") to publicly highlight consistent efforts.

3. **Addressing Systemic Challenges & Measurement Aversion**

- Consistency Scorecards: Develop performance metrics that explicitly track and reward process adherence and proactive, consistent behaviors, not just outputs.

- Standardize Processes: Invest in clear, documented processes and training from onboarding onwards to ensure a shared understanding of consistent execution.

- Measurement as Feedback: Reframe measurement not as judgment, but as essential data for growth and refinement.

- Process Improvement Loops: Create channels for employees to provide feedback on processes, fostering ownership and reducing measurement aversion.

4. The Role of Leadership in Cultivating Consistency

- Patience & Persistence: Recognize that building consistent habits is a long-term endeavor requiring patience (e.g., the "66 days" average).

- Lead by Example ("Walk the Talk"): Leaders must personally demonstrate commitment to consistent habits and process adherence.

- Consistent Communication: Relentlessly reinforce the strategic importance of steady effort.

- Protect Consistent Efforts: Shield teams focused on long-term improvements from constant short-term pressures.

- Coach for **Consistency**: Make **consistency** a regular topic in performance discussions and coaching.

5. The Power of Embedded Consistency

- Commitment to Process: True consistency is about a steadfast commitment to the process of improvement, not just achieving isolated goals.

- Compounding Effect: Small, regular actions, when sustained, compound into significant, transformative results.

- Ingrained Reflex: The ultimate goal is for consistent action to become less of a conscious effort and more of an automatic, ingrained way of operating.

The Final Inning

Principles That Transcend the Game

"It ain't over till it's over" - Yogi Berra

The famous Yogi Berra quote perfectly captures a fundamental truth about both baseball and life: success isn't over until the final out. Just as a baseball team can mount an incredible comeback in the ninth inning, your journey of growth and achievement continues throughout your entire career – and life.

As we conclude our exploration of *The Consistency Effect*, having just explored the common roadblocks that can derail our best efforts and the strategies to dismantle them, let's reflect on how reliable actions transform into remarkable results, not through spectacular home runs, but through the steady accumulation of singles and doubles that ultimately win the game of business and life.

The Power of Persistent Growth Many professionals assume their development journey ends once they reach a certain level of success. They believe they can coast on accumulated knowledge and experience. This mindset is like a baseball team deciding to stop practicing because they're ahead in the standings. The reality is that true masters never stop growing.

Looking back at my journey from wannabe rock star to CEO, every experience, even those that felt like strikeouts at the time, were lessons that contributed to a broader education. That young drummer who practiced relentlessly, investing thousands of hours perfecting his craft, unknowingly laid the foundation for a crucial life lesson: success isn't about one perfect performance; it's about many performances delivered over time.

When I abandoned my rock star dreams to return to university, it felt like failure. Yet the same discipline that had me practicing drums translated to my studies, transforming me from a mediocre student to someone on the Dean's Honor Roll. The passion I once poured into music found new expression in business innovation, team building and organizational transformation.

Your Consistency Playbook: Key Lessons for Lasting Success

Through both my personal journey and the concepts we've explored together, several core principles emerge that can guide your own path to sustainable success:

1. Embrace the Power of Singles and Doubles

The most enduring achievements aren't built on occasional breakthroughs but on consistent daily excellence. Throughout my business career – from summer student at A.E. Lepage to CEO at Sotheby's International Realty Canada – I've experienced both spectacular successes and humbling setbacks. Each transition and challenge reinforced the power of small, daily victories compounded over time, especially when fighting the allure of the grand slam or the internal bias for quick wins.

2. Be Mindful of the GRAND SLAM Elements

Success requires multiple elements working in harmony: Great Ideas, Resilience, Ambition, Network, Discipline, Skills, Luck, Action, and Mentorship. Assess your journey through this lens: Where are you strongest? Where do you need development? Rather than pursuing perfection in every area, focus on strengthening your weakest links while leveraging your natural strengths.

3. Master Adaptable Consistency

Perhaps the most powerful skill I've developed is maintaining consistency while constantly evolving. From musician to CEO, I've held true to fundamental principles while completely reinventing their application. This paradoxical ability – being simultaneously reliable and innovative – becomes increasingly valuable in today's rapidly changing landscape and is our best defense against the systemic challenges and neural biases that pull us off course. Consistency isn't just about doing the same things repeatedly; it's about maintaining foundational principles while evolving their application for changing circumstances.

4. Transform Setbacks into Future Foundations

Every disappointment contains the seeds of future growth. The persistence that kept me practicing despite my music teacher's doubts, the resilience that helped me bounce back from setbacks, and the adaptability that enabled multiple career transitions – these weren't separate lessons but different expressions of the same fundamental principle. When faced with apparent failure, ask yourself:

"What skills am I gaining that might serve me elsewhere?"

5. Invest in Relationships Consistently

Your network isn't something you build when you need it. It's something you nurture continually. Life beyond the boardroom provided some of my most powerful lessons. Finding love again with Tanya taught me that life's greatest gifts often arrive in unexpected packages. Our relationship flourished not through a single event but through consistent acts of friendship, support, and, ultimately, love.

6. Practice Intentional Work-Life Integration

Success isn't just about professional achievements. It's about consistently nurturing your authentic self beyond any title or role. Be intentional about protecting time for personal growth, maintaining genuine relationships, and pursuing interests outside of business. This integration hasn't just made me a better leader; it's made me a better person, partner, and father.

7. Implement Clear Performance Frameworks

Establish transparent metrics for your own success and that of your team. Define what meeting expectations truly means and what exceeding them requires. This clarity transforms vague aspirations into achievable targets and provides a roadmap for continuous improvement, helping to counter measurement aversion and ensure systemic support for consistent effort.

8. Maintain Strategic Focus Despite Distractions

Your ability to say "no" to good opportunities so you can say "yes" to great ones will determine your long-term success. Develop clear criteria for what aligns with your core priorities and recognize that productive anxiety about missed opportunities often signals healthy focus.

9. Balance Experiences and Accumulation

Recognize that different life stages offer unique opportunities that won't return. Create a deliberate strategy that considers not just financial resources but physical capabilities and life circumstances, prioritizing experiences that matter most.

10. Commit to Excellence in Every Interaction

Make "Be Legendary" your personal standard, delivering exceptional experiences regardless of context. This builds a reputation and personal brand that creates lasting differentiation.

Your Legacy Beyond Achievement

Perhaps most importantly, remember that your legacy isn't just about your achievements – it's about the impact you have on others. Consistent excellence, even when it means pushing against the grain of short-term thinking or our own biases for quick wins, creates ripple effects that extend far beyond your immediate sphere. Your team members learn from your example, colleagues adopt your best practices, mentees carry your lessons forward, and organizations benefit from your contribution long after you've moved on.

This multiplier effect means your commitment to consistency doesn't just benefit you. It enriches the entire professional and personal ecosystem around you.

The Game Continues

If there's one final lesson I've learned through decades of business leadership, it's this: there's always another inning to play. Whether you're starting a new chapter, transitioning careers, facing unexpected setbacks, or pursuing fresh challenges, the principles of the Consistency Effect remain your most reliable guide.

One of the most challenging aspects of the Consistency Effect is maintaining your commitment to growth when circumstances change. The key is recognizing that each transition isn't an ending but an opportunity to apply your accumulated wisdom in new ways while remaining open to further growth.

The game isn't over until you decide to stop playing. Your journey can continue as long as you're willing to embrace new challenges, navigate the inevitable barriers with the strategies we've discussed, and remain committed to consistent excellence. Every setback contains the seeds of future success if you maintain your commitment to growth. Your next challenge isn't about hitting a home run; it's about showing up ready to get on base, advance your position, and keep moving forward.

Keep showing up. Keep learning. Keep contributing. And most importantly, keep growing.

To me, years of consistent performance leading to game-changing success is 'hitting it out of the park' and that is the essence of *The Consistency Effect.*

About the Author

Brad Henderson is a seasoned business leader with over four decades of experience spanning the real estate, information technology, and telecommunications sectors. His career is marked by a steadfast belief that exceptional organizations are built on the cornerstones of engaged leadership, empowered teams, continuous improvement, and unwavering client focus.

As a highly accomplished Leader, CEO and business strategist, Brad has consistently demonstrated his ability to drive bottom-line growth and achieve winning outcomes across various industries.

Brad is currently pursuing his passion for coaching and mentoring through his firm, The Consistency-Edge. Prior to his current role, Brad was a Managing Director of Cushman & Wakefield's Data Center Advisory Group. Under Brad's leadership, this specialized team has leveraged its expertise in risk analysis, portfolio strategy, strategic planning, and account management to oversee more than $1 billion in sales and lease transactions worldwide. Brad served as President and CEO of Sotheby's International Realty Canada and Dundee 360 Real Estate Development Corporation. In this capacity, he managed $5 billion in sales, a $100 million revenue stream and a workforce of 600 employees across 32 offices.

Brad's leadership journey included a stint as Senior Regional Managing Director at CBRE, where he oversaw operations generating $150 million in revenue and managed 1,200 employees across Canada and the North Central United States. As President and COO of Gibraltar Solutions, an IT solutions provider, he specialized in virtualization, remote access, and cloud computing. Earlier in his career, Brad held the position of Group Vice President & General Manager at TELUS Communications, where he was responsible for three groups with a combined revenue of $800 million and a workforce of 6,000.

A firm believer in the importance of corporate governance, Brad earned his ICD.D designation from the Institute of Corporate Directors in 2017. His commitment to community service and industry leadership is evident in his numerous board positions. Currently, he serves as Chair of the Board of Directors for the Marco Island Marina Association. His past board memberships include TELUS International, CSDC Systems Inc., and Ambergris Solutions Inc.

Brad's dedication to civic engagement is exemplified by his leadership roles in various committees for the Toronto Board of Trade and CivicAction.

Throughout his career, Brad has consistently demonstrated a unique ability to navigate complex business landscapes, drive innovation, and foster growth. His wealth of experience and proven track record make him a respected voice in the business community and a valuable asset to any organization fortunate enough to benefit from his leadership.

In *The Consistency Effect: How to Turn Reliable Actions into Remarkable Results*, Brad leverages his extensive experience to provide practical insights and advice on achieving long-term success through consistent, reliable actions. His book celebrates the importance of everyday achievements, emphasizing how consistent singles and doubles can lead to a fulfilling and successful life, both personally and professionally.

Website: www.consistency-edge.com
Email: bradhenderson@me.com
LinkedIn: https://www.linkedin.com/in/bradjhenderson/

Transform Your Leadership Journey with The Consistency-Edge

After four decades of leading organizations through transformative change, I now help executives and first-time CEOs turn potential into sustained success. Drawing from real-world experience across multiple industries and organizations of various sizes, I offer personalized executive coaching that combines proven business principles with practical implementation strategies.

Who I Work With

- Senior executives and first-time CEOs.

- Leaders of organizations with 50+ employees.

- Professionals navigating significant career transitions.

- Executives facing organizational transformation challenges.

Core Focus Areas

- Transition from operational expert to strategic leader.

- Build and lead high-performing teams.

- Drive organizational change and digital transformation.

- Develop authentic leadership style.

- Create sustainable work-life integration.

The Consistency-Edge Approach

Building on the principles outlined in The Consistency Effect, my coaching methodology focuses on:

- Converting strategic vision into systematic execution.

- Building sustainable leadership practices.

- Creating measurable, achievable milestones.

- Developing consistent habits for lasting success.

- Implementing proven business frameworks.

Why Choose Me

- Four decades of senior leadership experience.

- Successful transitions across multiple industries.

- Practical, tested solutions that deliver results.

- Focus on systematic, sustainable improvement.

- Balance of strategic vision and tactical execution.

Getting Started

Begin your leadership transformation with a complimentary 30-minute strategy session. During this focused conversation, we'll:

- Identify your specific leadership challenges

- Explore potential solutions

- Determine if we're the right fit.

- Outline next steps for your development.

Connect With Me

Website: www.consistency-edge.com
Email: bradhenderson@me.com

LinkedIn: https://www.linkedin.com/in/
bradjhenderson/

Transform your leadership potential into consistent, sustainable success. Book your complimentary strategy session today.

Acknowledgements

Like singles and doubles in baseball, no book comes into being through a single swing. This work represents the collective wisdom, support, and encouragement of many who've stepped up to the plate alongside me.

My deep gratitude goes to Beth Wareham, my editor and self-proclaimed "blonde hammer," whose unique ability to simultaneously cheerlead and challenge, transformed these pages from rambling thoughts into a coherent narrative.

To my beta readers, Kyle Dennhardt, John O'Bryan, and Anne Hayes, thank you for the enormous efforts you put into making the book better.

Throughout my career, I've been fortunate to learn first-hand from some extraordinary leaders: William Dimma, Darren Entwistle, Rowland Fleming, Doug Henderson, Richard McIntyre, William Moore, Joe Natale, Basile Papaevangelou, and Jeffrey Puritt, each of whom has contributed to my professional growth.

Several key individuals played pivotal roles in my professional transitions. Paul Goldman, the true "Moneyball" owner of Arqana (and Ian Gragtmans who introduced us), gave me my first break in transitioning industries, demonstrating that talent can transfer across fields. Kerry Shapansky's networking prowess led to my role at Sotheby's International Realty Canada, and whose ongoing friendship, coaching, and support continue to be phenomenal.

Karla Congson served as my digital sherpa, guiding me through the world of social media and the evolving landscapes of AI. Her Agentiiv platform proved instrumental in the creation of this book.

Tony Robbins has shaped my journey through his writings, recordings, videos, and live performances. Our unforgettable 90-minute conversation had a powerful, and lasting impact on both my personal and professional life.

To John O'Bryan, my most impactful mentor, your influence, whether through direct guidance or by example, has fundamentally shaped who I've become as a leader and a person. You are truly remarkable and, without doubt, the most honorable person I've ever met.

The Nature of Mentorship

Life brings us mentors in different ways, each serving unique purposes in our journey. Some enter our lives briefly but powerfully, illuminating specific paths and imparting crucial lessons. Their timely presence and sage advice have shaped pivotal moments, steering me toward growth and self-discovery.

Others walk alongside us through seasons of challenge or triumph. To these companions whose insights have left an indelible mark on my character and worldview, I extend my deepest appreciation.

To the precious few who have been steadfast pillars throughout my lifetime, words cannot fully express my gratitude. Your unwavering presence, unconditional love, and enduring wisdom have been the bedrock upon which I've built my dreams and aspirations.

I am equally indebted to those mentors I've never met in person, but whose influence has transcended time and space. Through your written words, stirring lectures, and timeless wisdom, you have ignited my curiosity and illuminated paths of possibility. Your legacy reminds us that mentorship knows no bounds and inspiration can flourish across generations.

A Personal Note

Most emphatically, I am eternally grateful to my extraordinary life coach, confidante, and soulmate – my wife, Tanya. You embody unwavering support and boundless love. More than just my best friend, you are my compass, guiding me through storms of doubt and calm seas of success with equal grace. Your belief in me has been transformative, empowering me to step beyond my comfort zone and discover vast potential. Your never-ending love reminds me of our partnership's beauty and the strength born of mutual support and shared dreams.

Looking Forward

To all my mentors – named and unnamed, known and unknown – this book stands as a tribute to your profound influence and celebrates mentorship's ripple effect. May your shared wisdom, kindness, and inspiration continue touching countless lives and fostering legacies of growth, compassion, and achievement. May this book inspire others to seek mentorship, embrace guidance, and become beacons of wisdom for future generations.

thank you

Thank you for reading my book!

Dear Reader,

You made it! Thanks for sticking with me through these pages. I hope they brought you some insights, a few laughs, and maybe even a spark of inspiration. Sharing these stories and lessons has been an incredible journey, and it means a lot that you chose to be a part of it.

Now, if I could ask a quick favour: if you enjoyed the book, would you mind leaving a positive review on Amazon or Goodreads. It would truly make my day, and it's one of the best ways to help others find this book and maybe spark their own adventures. Your review might just be the encouragement someone else needs to give them permission to break from routine and empower them to make the change they need.

Best,
Brad

MY GIFT TO YOU

I am so glad you're here!

As my Gift to you, get FREE access the Audiobook of **The Consistency Effect: How to Turn Reliable Actions into Remarkable Results** by scanning the QR Code below or visiting

https://www.consistency-edge.com/pages/shop